Train Lord

Train Lord

OLIVER MOL

MICHAEL JOSEPH

MICHAEL JOSEPH

UK | USA | Canada | Ireland | Australia
India | New Zealand | South Africa

Michael Joseph is part of the Penguin Random House group of companies
whose addresses can be found at global.penguinrandomhouse.com

First published 2022
001

Copyright © Oliver Mol, 2022

The moral right of the author has been asserted

Set in 13.5/16pt Garamond MT Std
Typeset by Jouve (UK), Milton Keynes
Printed and bound in Great Britain by Clays Ltd, Elcograf S.p.A.

The authorized representative in the EEA is Penguin Random House Ireland,
Morrison Chambers, 32 Nassau Street, Dublin D02 YH68

A CIP catalogue record for this book is available from the British Library

HARDBACK ISBN: 978-0-241-52506-7

www.greenpenguin.co.uk

For Holly, for everything

To discuss oneself is to invite disaster. Never give an interview. Never, under any conditions, write the story of your life. And, it would be better not to write poetry either. Even fiction can incriminate you. The safest procedure, it goes without saying, is to write nothing at all.

Paul Bowles, *An Exemplary Essay*

Train Lord

The first day of train school our teacher asked us what we would do if we were on the train and we had to go to the toilet, and we'd already had our break. For a while, no one spoke. Then Susie said, Shit in a bag, sir. Yeah. Probably shit in a bag. Good on ya, Suze, our teacher said. The shit in a bag approach. A classic. Then we went around the room and said our names and where we'd come from and a fun fact about us too. Ed said he'd worked in logistics and sailed around the world with the Navy in his youth, and Zayd had been a transit cop with a baby on the way. But now it was my turn and I didn't know what to say. I didn't want to talk about the migraine or how I'd failed as a writer. I didn't want to talk about pain. So I said my name was Oliver and flipped my wrist frypan-style. I winked and said that I loved to cook.

***

Five months of train school? What the hell did you learn? Sam asked. We learned about the railway, the different trains, the S sets and K sets and C sets and T sets and M sets and H sets and A sets and B sets. We learned how to communicate with bell signals and where to locate the fire extinguishers and how to administer first aid. We learned the Sydney Trains Network, every station in order, and what platforms, if any, a train could terminate on. We learned how to take a train apart and put it back together, and how to drive the train in case the driver became incapacitated. We learned how to prepare and how to terminate a train, how to test for faults, and how to talk, phonetically, on the radio, as if we were in the army, like my dad taught me long ago. We learned how to evacuate trains, safely, methodically, and we learned to follow rules. We learned the correct procedures for opening windows and climbing ladders and wearing backpacks and the correct paths to walk from the station to the train yard. We learned which signals were permissive and which were absolute and which would remain red, fixed, no matter what. We learned to slow down, to not think, or to think only about what we had learned; we learned how to stop.

And I remembered how to breathe.

We were shown how to wake drunken people passed out on the train and we were given the number for security and told about the guards who had been assaulted late at night. We were told to watch out for spitters and we were told of the frequent suicides and we were told to watch out for fights. We were told about the snakes, especially at Leppington, and we were told that none of this was a joke. We were told about the drugs tests and the alcohol tests, and we watched videos, filmed in the 90s, about the trains that had derailed and the people who had died because someone, somewhere, had failed to follow the rules.

We learned to make announcements, to stay calm; we learned to be rocks. We learned that in life and work the waves would come and the waves would crash and people would yell and call us names, but we wouldn't care because we were stable and dependable and when the waves were gone we were still there because we were rock people now. We learned all this and five months later we passed exams and were given shirts and pants and hats and whistles and belts and vests and flags and backpacks and shoes and belts and keys. We worked a 24-hour roster, seven days a week, 365 days a year. We were given train diagrams that told us where to stop and when to have lunch and when and where our shifts would end. And there was something beautiful about changing, about not writing, or not thinking, or thinking very little, about wearing a uniform and being told what to do.

Congratulations, our teacher said on the last day of school. You've all won the lottery. I've been with the railway for forty-seven years, and I've never worked a day in my life.

***

On my first shift, there was a suicide. I went to Hornsby to relieve the guard; his train had cut someone in half. Fucking useless pricks always offing themselves around Christmas, he said. Want my advice? Don't look at the body. So I sat on the train while emergency services cleaned up the blood and the limbs and the mess, and when the body wheeled past I tried to look away, but I couldn't. I had to see the body wrapped in a white sheet on a stretcher, and I had to see the way their legs poked one way and their arms poked another. I had to see the sun and I had to see the sky, the blood drying beneath it, and I had to imagine his parents or friends or siblings when they got the call. I had to know what that moment looked like, that this wasn't just an idea, that this was final, that this was real. After I took the train to the sheds, I burst into tears.

When I was a writer, or unemployed, living at Toby's house, in his bed, he sat me down and said: Oliver. You need to get your shit together. Get a job. This is no way to live your life. And so we spent the following hours drinking Toby's rum and snorting Toby's cocaine, looking at all the ways it might be possible for me to grow up. We looked at advertising jobs and public relations jobs and copywriting jobs. The following day I updated my LinkedIn. I wrote cover letters, emails. Once, absurdly, I even arrived unannounced at the door of a creative agency, my résumé in a manila folder. I was twenty-five, then, and on the rare occasion I received an interview, I would make the mistake of telling the truth. I would say that I did not have a business degree or a communications degree but that I did have one of the most useless degrees of all: a creative writing degree. I would say that I did not have any formal copywriting or advertising or marketing experience, but explain that the rights to my first book had been sold, and that I'd been published over fifty times in Australia and overseas, and that I'd built a following for myself online (now, largely defunct). Then I would smile and leave, realizing what I'd suspected all along: that no one gave a shit how many pieces of fiction or non-fiction you had published, that, in the end, the best-case scenario for Australian letters was a life of obscurity and critique, and perhaps a book or two, a couple of writers' festivals, but rarely, or in my case never, a living or a job.

With the trains everything changed.

***

Apart from those cramped platform meal rooms where we ate next to those horrific bathrooms, where wafts of shit would mix with sweat and microwaved meat or vegetables or curry, the job was one of the best many of us had known. So long as I had something to occupy me between stations, I didn't mind working weekends or on my days off. The money you could earn – at least to me – was astonishing. When all was well, when there were no delays and management wasn't calling to ask why you lost two minutes between Hornsby and Waitara, when there were no medical emergencies or fights or needle scares or fatalities or masturbators or drunks or screaming children or spitters or members of the public saying, apropos of nothing, 'Fuck you', or, 'Your network is a piece of shit', or, 'You're late', Sydney passed outside our windows with a tranquillity that I had not known before. G'day mate, I'd say, relieving a guard at Central or Lidcombe or Blacktown. How are ya? Living the dream, mate, they would inevitably reply. Living the bloody dream.

But these, too, were the days when the migraine would, inexplicably, return leaving me unable to look at screens and write or read. So one morning I walked to Optus on George Street and told the sales attendant that I wanted the cheapest phone they had. You're going to want internet, she said. No internet! What about Instagram? Uber? No Instagram! No Uber! I told her I wanted a phone that made calls and sent texts and played the radio and recorded my voice.

Can you hear me? What? Can you hear me? No. After a while my family and I just laughed: the phone barely worked. It dropped out every ten seconds, but I could send texts and look at the screen, could communicate and be heard. Eventually my family encouraged me to try recording stories on what we now called my burner phone. Burnie Sanders, my brother would say. Feel the burn! Give him the business! And so I would make my announcements, then hit record, stopping to open and close the train doors before departing, and hitting record again. The process was frustrating, time-consuming, but it gave me something to do, and after roughly a month I produced my first story.

During train school, the trainer wanted to show us the points. So we went down to the train yard and looked at the mechanical installations that guide the trains from one track to another. The trainer told us a week earlier someone had pulled the points when the train was travelling across them, and the train derailed. What do you think about that? Pretty shit, I said. Fuckin' oath it's shit. The trainer told us there was a process for everything. All injuries were preventable. Even snake bites. Snakes? Fuckin' oath, snakes. He told us there were king browns everywhere.

Just the other day another trainer had told us about the time he found a king brown on a seat. King brown? someone had said. What's that? It's a human fucking shit, isn't it? But now we weren't talking about shit. We were talking about snakes.

You gotta be careful, he said. The brown snakes: they'll chase ya, then kill ya.

The trainer told us to be prepared for anything. He told us about the accidents, about the suicides. He told us there was nearly one a day, but the tabloids didn't report it. He told us Father's Day was the worst. Followed by Christmas. More cunts die on the railway than the roads. Just look around. Everything can kill you.

So I looked around and saw all the trains and train lines and overhead wires, and I looked even further and saw all the cars and roads and people. Then I looked even further and saw Maria, whom I used to love, and I saw myself too. I saw that we were smiling. We were smiling because we knew you couldn't see the real killers.

Then the trainer pulled the points lever and the tracks changed from one route to another. The job's easy, he said. But sometimes shit fucks up. You gotta be tough. He told me his wife died of leukaemia a few years back. Then he lit a cigarette. He laughed and said he knew she'd be watching. He knew she'd be mad. He'd promised he'd quit but now it didn't matter. Every dart, he said, inhaling, brings me closer to her.

At some point we returned to the path and walked to the platform. We sat at Waterfall station and waited for the train. And I knew there was no logic to anything. Because the very things that killed you could also bring you home.

***

One afternoon, while waiting for our trains, I began talking to a guard about the usual: how much of the shift they had left, how long they had been on the job, what they had done before when he moved a bit closer, lowered his voice and said, Do you ever get lonely? He told me that since he'd graduated he'd barely seen his wife. He lived north, somewhere on the Central Coast, and between her day shifts and his night shifts and the commute, he was struggling to find time to sleep, to see his kids, to relax. There's just no quality time any more, he said. I told him I knew what he meant.

In truth, I did not know what he meant. I was single; I lived in Darlington, 500 metres from Redfern station, three minutes from Central by train. I did not have to think for others, nor did I have a mortgage, or any debt beyond my enormous university one – compiled from years of useless degrees and indecision.

I told him I didn't know how he did it, commuting an hour and a half each way. We required eleven hours between shifts, but assuming, for example, that he finished at 2.30 a.m., he would, at best, if he had a car, be home around 3.45 a.m., though if he had to rely on public transport, it would be closer to five in the morning. Then, he would sleep six or seven or eight hours only to wake in time for the return commute in the event that he had a 3.30 p.m. start. Of course, a shift like this was rare, but not unheard of, and as a new guard, one had to wait until a line opened up on the roster, until one had accrued enough seniority, which only happened when someone died, or quit. Only then could a guard transition to a permanent line that allowed them to sleep, to see their partners, to live a life of their own rather than facilitating the movement and direction of others.

Maybe in four or five years I can move to Hornsby, he said. Or maybe I'll become an intercity guard and get stationed at Gosford for Newcastle. But that was another thing: there were rumours intercity guards would be made redundant soon. Of course the bosses had been threatening to remove guards for the past thirty years; there were always rumours on the railway – when we started we were told, if you haven't heard a rumour by 9 a.m. . . . make one up. All around us, the world was changing; automation, we knew, was coming, and it was no secret the current government and Transport Minister resented the power

9

that guards and drivers had over them and their city. But at that moment, my fellow guard wasn't thinking about job security; he was thinking about his wife. I heard there's a high rate of divorce on the job, he said.

It was only a few weeks later that I started to feel lonely too. I'd been working for close to a year, mostly evenings and nights. I would start around five or six or seven and finish between one and three in the morning. I liked those shifts; I had my days free: to swim, to climb, but now I was on mornings and after eight consecutive days my world had begun to shrink, to change. Waking, initially, at one or two in the morning had seemed barbaric, but interesting. There was a van that would pick me up close to my house at the Redfern station car park and take me to Central but most of the time I chose to walk. I liked walking: past the Glengarry, nodding at Ollie or whoever was having staff drinks after hours; through Prince Alfred Park, the park that many years earlier I had done push-ups in, or cried in, or had simply lain in, when I had the migraine, when I couldn't do anything at all. I would walk through that park in the early morning listening to jazz, which now seems like a false, additional detail, the kind of detail added by an editor to seem cultural. But the truth is I did listen to jazz, and what occurred next happened too.

One morning around 6 a.m., halfway through my

shift and on my break, I burst into tears beneath the large clock at Central. These weren't little, push-them-back-in tears, but inconsolable-unable-to-breathe tears. I hurried around a corner, turned my back and cried into my shirt. I didn't know what was happening.

My phone rang. I felt a pang of anxiety that it was a manager calling to tell me I'd missed a train, that I'd been crying for so long I'd lost track of time. But it was my mum. She was awake, about to go for a run. Hey Oliver, she said. How are you? Not good, I managed to say, or almost say, after a while. I told her I felt lonely, that I spent all day in my own train compartment, in a tiny metal box, and that when I went home I was by myself too. I told her I tried to exercise to make myself feel better but inevitably I did that alone. I told her I didn't want to be by myself any more. I wanted connection, relationships, a normal job, a nine to five; I wanted to talk to people, to be heard. It's too much, I said, suddenly shaking from the lack of sleep, or from coffee, and then I said, I just feel so empty. I have to go to bed at five in the afternoon if I want eight hours of sleep, but it's still light outside; my housemates are having fun; I don't know how to do that; I don't know how to do anything any more. Then I burst into tears once more and said, I'm just sick of being alone.

Mum told me to slow down and she told me to breathe. Then she said something else but a train passed; its brakes screeched so loud that I recoiled, and I told her I couldn't hear her. Then I started apologizing, telling her I knew how pathetic it all sounded, that I shouldn't complain, that I was acting like a child, that I knew how lucky I was. And then I asked that absurd question we asked as children: if things would get better, if my body would heal; in the end I wanted to know if I would be able to work another job, a normal job, one that involved a computer; I wanted to know if I would be able to write again, perhaps not like I used to, but at least on paper, without pain; I wanted to know if I would be left behind.

Sometimes it felt like Sydney was a microcosm of the world, and the world was falling apart. One night, around 2 a.m., I was on break getting a kebab when this guy walked in asking for scissors. Got any scissors? Need to get this thing out of my ear. Then he showed me his ear – there was a headphone jack pushed all the way in. It was like one side of him had sealed up, and I thought he looked like a doll. Stupid headphone jack, he kept saying. Then he grabbed a plastic fork someone had left on the counter and tried to fork the headphone jack out, but it wouldn't come. Eventually he turned to me and asked me what I reckoned. I reckon you should go to hospital, I said. Yeah, hospital, he said. Naa. Maccas will have scissors. Then he threw the fork back on the container and walked away.

I didn't have many friends at work, and this suited me fine. I was lonely, but I wasn't there to make friends – I was there to go around and around for as long as I needed to figure out my problems, and to work out if it might be possible to love myself again.

Another afternoon. After spending an incredible amount of money on a mouth guard at the dentist that, I was told, was necessary, would prevent my teeth from clenching and perhaps, over time, even alleviate the pain in my jaw and head, I rode the train to Fairfield and ate lunch at an Iraqi restaurant, several blocks behind the station. The dentist's assistant was a wiry, likeable guy with firm posture, and I had told him about my jaw pain, but also about my neck pain and shoulder pain, about the headaches that came and went, and he had told me about his pain too, how, sometimes, when he returned home he could barely walk, that he would lie for hours on his back on a tennis ball trying to make it all go away. But, he said, I've got this guy. You've got to see my guy. He's a chiropractor. And he works miracles. And so he wrote his name and he wrote his number, and I sat in the restaurant eating a kebab staring at the paper thinking about all the miracles I heard about when I was young: about Jesus walking on water and turning water into wine, about making the blind man see, and right then I made a prayer, or a deal. I said, if you'll help me; if you'll make the pain go away, I swear to God, to you, I'll do anything you want. And so the chiropractor bent and twisted and pressed and adjusted, and my body stretched and cracked and popped, and for a while I even kept thinking: holy shit, laughing, or at least smiling, because it had worked. But then, on the train home the pain returned. My neck tightened and my back tightened, my head throbbed, and it was like the whole world had shrunk too. I wiped my eyes and put on my sunglasses. You stupid fuck, I thought, wasting your money. For thinking, believing, that you might be okay.

I only drink two days of the year: when it's my birthday, and when it's not my birthday, the driver said, and then he burst into laughter and shook his head. You young blokes don't get humour. We were walking through the train yard at Flemmo on our way to prep a train. So what's your story? Been out long? Bit over a year, I said. Thought you looked a bit wet behind the ears. I've been on the rails for thirty-five years. Course, before that I was driving freight. Fuck me dead, that was a job. Back when I was a young fella we'd drive days on end, just the desert and your mate and the sun and your feet on the dash. Mind you, that was all before drug testing. I don't smoke any more, barely drink, he said, winking, except for those two days a year. Anyway, got a missus? Naa, I said. Wouldn't worry about it. Even an ugly bas-tard like you should be able to get someone to marry ya. It was three in the morning, a full moon; we walked single file between trains and the world droned. What did you do before? For crust? Couple things, I said. I worked in pubs; I was a tour guide, an usher; for a while, I was even a writer. A writer! Plenty of money in that racket. Goldmine, I said. I'm just doing this for fun. Me too, he said. Then we climbed into the crew compartment at the front of the train. I used to paint, he said after a while. Not, like, seriously. Not professionally. But I wasn't bad. In the end, though, I had to decide: pub or painting; girls or painting; making money or painting. It was just too hard. I didn't love it. It became a pain. It became a pain, I repeated. Yeah, that's more or less what happened to me.

***

It's nothing serious, the doctor had said, years earlier, staring at the MRI or CAT scan or whatever test my GP had recommended. In fact, the doctor said, there's nothing wrong with you at all. What is it that you do? I knew the doctor meant: what do you do for work, but I couldn't help thinking about what it was I did with my time. I take codeine pills. I cry when no one is watching. I pretend that everything is okay. Then I said, I'm a writer, or I was a writer. I can't look at a book or a page or a computer or a screen. Why? Because it hurts. Hurts where? In my head. Do you make any money from writing? A little, I said. Not really. The doctor considered this, then said, Well I suggest you forget writing and find another career. The thought, until then, that I would give up writing had never occurred to me, and in the elevator I turned to Maria and said, Fuck that guy. But more silently, I thought, Fuck. She agreed, calling him names – a fuckhead, a loser – but on the train home, eyes closed, I knew I was just disappointed and angry with my body, with myself.

But the truth was I had been writing. Slowly, in pencil, in pen, on paper, in secret, between stations. If I wore my glasses, took frequent breaks and completed my exercises, I was, for a while, able to remain pain free, and occasionally, when I produced something I didn't hate, I would invite Sam and Taylah up to my room. I would read them small passages from a collection of papers I had titled *As Yet, Unfinished Novel.* I would read them stories that I wanted to forget but could not forget: small, fragmentary stories about Maria and me and the migraine and Sydney that, even now, I'm sure weren't translated properly, butchered somewhere between reality or so-called reality, between my imagination and the page. I would read these stories quickly, initially with excitement, though towards the end with embarrassment and shame – at what, exactly? I'm not sure, though I suspect that it had something to do with failure. It's very sad, Taylah said, one time when I finished. I smiled because that was the sort of writing I was attracted to then, that stupid sort of writing that meant I was a serious writer – writing that pretended to be something else, a little comedic, before breaking your heart.

After Maria left, I sat outside my house and waited for her to call. I sat under a streetlight and kept telling Siri to call Maria. I couldn't look at my phone and I didn't know what to do. Hey Siri . . . call Maria. Sorry, I don't understand. Siri . . . call Maria. Call Nakia? Please . . . call Maria. Calling Maria. Then I got her voicemail. Then I got her voicemail again. Then I got her voicemail again. Then I got her voicemail again. Then I asked if she was coming home. I said, Please come home . . . please. I told her I was an idiot but she used to love this idiot and maybe she still did. I told her I loved her and I was sorry and that I needed her. I told her I was proud she was seeing a psychologist and I promised I'd get help too. Then I promised if she came home I'd tell her a story that would make her laugh. I told her I wasn't going to tell her now but if she came home I would. Then I said, Just . . . please come home, and I hung up the phone.

For a while I sat on the kerb. Every few minutes, I walked on to the street to check if she was there. Then I saw someone walking up the street. I yelled out, Maria, but the person didn't say anything. So I yelled, Maria, again. But it wasn't Maria. It was my housemate. She asked what I was doing. Oh nothing, I said. Waiting for a mate. Are you . . . okay? Oh yeah, I said. Yeah? Yeah.

So my housemate went inside and I stayed, waiting for Maria to come. I thought about the nights we lay together and how she told me to visualize my successes. She told me no one, not even scientists, knew how the brain really worked. And then she said that even though you can't read or write, your imagination is still yours. She told me if we tried hard enough I could send the migraines away. She told me the brain was the UFO of the body, which made us aliens too.

So I closed my eyes and visualized her walking towards me. I practised the funny story I was going to tell her. I practised what I was going to say. I practised: You know how I'm an idiot? Well, after you left I met Arnie at the Lord Gladstone. We did a bunch of ketamine and, somehow, I inhaled a cigarette. I smoked, then did a bump. Smoked, then did a bump. Then I inhaled so hard the cigarette was gone. I practised: You know how I swallowed a cigarette? Well, the cigarette lodged in my throat, so I ran to the bathroom and skulled a beer I found next to the pisser. I imagined her laughing, and I imagined the whole world laughing.

Then I practised talking out loud because I didn't want to be alone. I opened my eyes and waited for her to come down the street. I waited for us to return upstairs and for me to lie face down on my pillow and for her to watch *Adventure Time*. I waited for the voices to come out of her laptop and for her to tell me what the characters were doing. Nothing happened. Then I tasted the cigarette inside me and I picked the ketamine from my nose and I tasted the bile I'd vomited earlier on.

I went inside and tried to have a shower but the water was cold so I returned to bed and waited for the hot water too. Then I got under my covers and went into a tiny ball. I pretended I was the cigarette, and I smiled because I knew one day everything would end. I knew I'd be shat out and the pain would be gone and I would be gone too. I knew life was just a game, and that game was called: waiting. And I knew there was nothing special about any of this. I knew we were the same boring characters the world had met a billion times before. I knew no one cared. And I knew I would have to stop caring too. I knew the secret to getting by in this world was to care as little as possible. I knew if I could stop caring then everything would be okay.

But I couldn't.

I can't.

I still remember our walks. Not that we liked walking, but walking was free and we had nothing else to do. One day I took some muscle relaxants and we walked towards Newtown, then Enmore, then Marrickville. We didn't really have a goal, an end point, and by the time we reached Marrickville station we were tired and hungry. But I didn't mind. I told her walking was good – this was what people did. I told her it was like we were a real couple, a modern couple, one of those couples who exercised together then returned home and made love on beds with the fresh sheets. I said, Talking 'bout FRESH sheets! and then I said, Besides, couples who train together, remain together, and I smiled a big, stupid smile. I was high.

This is bullshit, Maria said. I'm hungry. We have no money. And I hate walking. So we stood outside the train station and had an argument about walking. Then we sat on a bench and had an argument about food. Then she told me a train was coming in a few minutes and she would be on it. She told me she wasn't walking home and that the ticket inspectors could go fuck themselves and I could fuck myself too. So she went to leave but I grabbed her hand and begged her to stay. She said she hated walking, especially with me. She said I walked too fast. She told me she wasn't a suitcase. She wasn't just some dead weight that I could pull around. I told her I was sorry and that I loved her and I'd get more shifts and that maybe soon the migraines would go away. I told her I'd stop crying, that I'd be strong. Then I made a joke about all the push-ups I'd been doing and I flexed and said that even though my head was fucked, daddy still had that sweet bod. But she wasn't interested in daddy's sweet bod; she was walking away.

So I walked after her and said I'd go with her if I could. She told me she knew. Then I said, Just . . . don't get caught 'cause we can't afford the fine, and she told me she didn't care. She told me she didn't care about the muscle relaxants and the painkillers I was taking, or the computers and phones and books I couldn't look at, or the messages I couldn't send, or the windows I couldn't look out of, or the lights I couldn't see. She said, And maybe the doctors are right. Maybe there is nothing wrong with you. Maybe it is all in your head. Then she disappeared around the corner and I yelled, Wait. I yelled that we had to stick together and then I ran after her and yelled, Please. But she just walked up the stairs. I put my hands on my head and tried to breathe. I breathed and I breathed and then I began to cry. I knew I was the dead weight, the suitcase, and as her train pulled away I thought: Please, please, please don't leave me behind.

Six months working on this essay, and I'm still not telling it right. Because I'm not telling you about the passengers we helped and the announcements we made and how vital we were, are, to the safe running of the train. I'm not telling you about the grown men, women, we found, trashed, spread out on seats, carriage floors, and platforms at the end of the line unable to pronounce their own names. I'm not telling you about the police we contacted and the ambulances we called for the men with bad hearts and the women who had been punched and about the emergency brakes we pulled when people fell between the platform and the train. I'm not telling you how we were as young as eighteen and as old as eighty-four and how some colleagues died and others retired and even others got divorced. I'm not telling you about the dark circles that appeared under our eyes while we said, Are you all right, mate? as bodies were cleaned from the rails.

But that's not even the half of it, because I'm not telling

you about the elderly couples we saw helping one another along platforms and the kids we saw playing peek-a-boo with their reflections and the fathers who spent entire Sundays with their disabled sons: he knows the timetable and all the trains, one father told me. He loves riding the network, which means it's my favourite thing too.

I'm not telling you about the jokes, those beautiful dark jokes that, perhaps, were never jokes at all. I'm not telling you about the girl who pinned a suicide note to the noticeboard at Werrington. The way I heard it, she said her goodbyes, went down to the track and put her head on the rail. Ten minutes passed, but there was no train. So she started getting angry. She kept muttering, Fucking Sydney Trains. But she was determined. So she laid her head back down, and waited another twenty minutes, but still, there was no train. Eventually, she returned to the station to see what the hold-up was, and next to her suicide note was a print-out that read: BUSES REPLACE TRAINS THIS WEEKEND BETWEEN WERRINGTON AND KINGSWOOD.

I'm not telling you about the ladies in wheelchairs at Olympic Park who turned to their carers and said, Fucking hurry it up, fuck ass, and how the carers laughed. And I'm not telling you how I started doing funny announcements to distract from my own demoralizing, unpredictable pain. I'm not telling you how I told people that Newtown was named after Isaac Newtown and how Como was named after the Holden Commodore. I'm not telling you how I told people that Rockdale was named after Dwayne 'The Rock' Johnson and that Kings

Cross should be renamed Kings Crossed-out. I'm not telling you how one day I said, Attention, customers . . . Next stop is Ashfield. But for all you singles out there, we call it PASHFIELD. I told all the singles if they were ready to mingle to raise their hands, and then I dared all the singles to make out. I said, GO ON! HAVE A KISS! – and then I did a psycho laugh and said, NAA . . . JUST KIDDING! OR AM I? And then I sat back and watched everyone on my little train security camera blushing and talking and laughing, and it was almost like we weren't on a train to the jobs we hated or the partners we should have left long ago. It was almost like no one was sad and no one was in pain and we were all smiling at how stupid the world was. And it seemed so improbable, then, that we would all be together, as beautiful and flawed and useless as one another, just trying to get somewhere, to move, to go home.

The New Year's Eve before I quit, I stood at the country end of platform 16, Central station, and wondered where all the people had gone: the station was deserted. When my train arrived the guard said, Just come in from Penrith. Caught two fuckers fucking. Filthy! Can't blame them though. What else are you gonna do twenty minutes to midnight, New Year's Eve on a ghost train to the city? Anyway, train's sweet. Happy New Year! and as we left, I waved, and she waved, and the station staff waved and then the world went black because we entered a tunnel. I did my announcements, told people where they were going, where they could change, and then I even wished them Happy New Year's too. I said, Happy New Year's, legends. Glad you ditched all your cool parties to spend it with me, but as I scanned the train on my security camera I counted eleven people, mostly men over the age of forty, sitting alone. We left Wynyard and emerged from the tunnel. The Sydney Harbour Bridge was clouded in smoke – 5.8 million dollars' worth of fireworks had exploded, and none of us could see a thing.

This Is Not A Love Story

When I started writing, really writing, I treated it like a sport, like basketball. It was 2008, and I practised my sentences in the way that I practised lay-ups: ferociously, and from first light until dusk. I told myself that if I wrote enough and believed enough then I might be able to convince others to believe it too. I told myself if I could build the muscle memory, train the neck and throat of my sentences, then one day I would be able to make them sing. I wanted to make things up and get paid for it. I wanted to create funny stories that connected people and ideas and places even if, in the end, they weren't funny at all.

I wrote my first short story: an obnoxious, highly plagiarized, boring attempt at Roald Dahl drafted over the course of two weeks at Glebe Library. I wrote it by hand and when the story was done I wrote it out again, word for word. The transcribing took hours and I called it my second draft. Never mind that nothing had changed. It didn't matter. It was about the feeling, the time, to just be there spending time with the work.

My girlfriend, then, was – is – an extremely talented artist who agreed to illustrate the stories. There were nine copies in all, and we sold them for $5 each at the East Sydney Hotel. The story would be worthless now, but the artist's work has appreciated considerably. This was back in 2010, which meant we were children: creative and hungry and ready to learn. I'd never spent much time around artists, real artists, but my girlfriend's father was an extremely successful one: a painter, a musician, a poet. So you want to be a writer? he asked one evening when the rest of the family had left the kitchen. Yes, I said, quickly, earnestly. Not a lot of money in that, he said, laughing, and then I laughed too, because he was right, and because the way I'd said yes seemed brash, sure, serious, but so absolutely indicative of what I wanted to become that laughter was all I could do. But then he stopped laughing and looked me in the eye. Well, he said. If you work hard and you have a whole lot . . . and I mean a whole lot of luck . . . maybe . . . just maybe . . . it might save your life. So here's $5. Good luck. I took the note and put it in my wallet. Thanked him profusely. Then had trouble looking him in the eye. It was the first time I'd ever been paid for my work. And it meant something, not so much the money, but the gesture, the permission: the permission to express ideas and to write, to share them, to converse and talk.

In 2018 I was asked by the *Sydney Review of Books* to review Tao Lin's *Trip: Psychedelics, Alienation and Change*. At first, I was confused. Surely, there was someone more qualified than me. My debut book, *Lion Attack!*, had been published in 2015, but since then I had hardly published anything at all: a couple of interviews, a story, a reflection on mental health and a memoriam to my cousin's suicide. In many ways, I had turned my back on literature, not by choice, but by force.

What happened to you? Luke Carman asked recently after a reading I had organized in Newtown. You were everywhere. And then you disappeared. I told him I had a migraine. A real knock-out. It lasted ten months. And I wanted to die.

In 2011 I began a degree in Creative Writing at RMIT in Melbourne. There were eighty of us, perhaps more, and I remember Francesca Rendle-Short stood in front of the cohort and said, The average wage of a writer in Australia is $13,000 a year. Look around. Statistically speaking, it's entirely probable that none of you will publish a book. So we looked around. We grinned. Surely not, we thought, or I thought. I'd read all *The Paris Review* interviews with the famous authors. I knew there were tricks. Surely, it was possible to write better, to write more, to earn more. So I worked. In the mornings, I wrote. And in my lunch breaks, I wrote. And, in the evenings or early mornings, after packing down the bar, I wrote too. I wrote a thousand words a day every day for three years and then I wrote some more. When I wasn't writing, I read. I treated it like a job. I became, I suppose, obsessed, the way I told myself I had to be if I wanted any success. I felt myself becoming something, someone. Not a writer, though. I was young, but I knew the first rule about writing was that you never called yourself a writer.

Besides, calling yourself a writer seemed serious, and seriousness terrified me. At readings I measured my success by laughs. One evening I read alongside the author and poet Josephine Rowe. Josephine and I later became friends, but at the time she didn't like my work; she thought it was crude and juvenile. She was correct. But that evening I read a serious piece about growing up in America and she came up to me and said, Your other work is rubbish, but that was quite good. I can't remember if she said that exactly, but I remember the sentiment, and it moved me. The work had been taken seriously, which meant that I had been taken seriously. I suppose, in the future, that would become a problem: that lack of demarcation between work and author, but at the time I celebrated.

The following writers changed me: Elizabeth Ellen, Tom Cho, Romy Ash, Sam Pink, Karl Taro Greenfeld, Tao Lin, Scott McClanahan.

These were young writers, some local, and at night I would stay up late trying to emulate their words. I would underline their sentences and write in the margins, making notes on voice, on what voice could do, on character, and how they made their sentences sing. These were HOLY SHIT moments: observing, for the first time, the way a sentence could leap from humour to sadness, the shift within a paragraph from the deadpan to absurd, or what seemed absurd to me, then. These were stories filled with life and love and want and desire and I knew it was special to encounter these teachers at the beginning of my career. Often, I would write with their books open in front of me like literary maps in case I got lost. I wonder, now, at what point this happens for other writers, when we stop reading for pleasure, but to view the magic trick, the nuts and bolts, the factory of it: when we read not to relax but to learn, to pull the red cloth aside.

Listen: sometimes I hate writing, but it's only because I'm scared, because a story told well has the power to break you.

***

Emilie Friedlander, writing in *The FADER*:

Alt Lit was literature that felt more in line with my life than anything I'd ever read in school. It was literature that actually captured what it felt like to be me, a person in her twenties who lives in a big city and wants to connect with other people and spends most of her time working (and socializing) on the internet. It didn't seem to obey any rules, other than a seeming faithfulness in its own recurring obsessions: sex, drug use, depression, loneliness, community. It collapsed lived experience into art, with a boldness that made you wonder whether there ever needed to be a difference in the first place.

An interview with Alejandro Zambra was published by *The Rumpus*:

> You can say that literature is about topics like love, death and all that, but I think there is only one topic that applies to all literature and that is belonging. There is a me, there is a we, there is an us, and we want to belong to it or we don't want to belong.

I believed, then, so passionately in that scene formerly known as Alt Lit, in the community and the work, in these people who I'd never met who even so felt like family. I'd rarely felt that sense of community in Australia, and I looked up to these people as teachers, as mentors. I'd never had a mentor, either, not really, other than Geoff Lemon and the late Kat Muscat: that extraordinary woman and editor who taught me so much. I remember one evening Kat and I shared a cigarette in the gutter outside a party. She asked me how I was, how my writing was going. And it seems silly, now, or maybe it doesn't, but I told her a story about a festival director who had humiliated me in front of a group of writers I'd admired. Fuck those arseholes, Kat said, her arm around me. Yeah, I said, sobbing, and then we were laughing, because I told her Katia and I had stolen a plant from the festival entrance in protest. It seemed ludicrous, suddenly, to play this game, to get noticed, to impress, to network, to publish in this tiny pocket of the world, the Melbourne literary scene, that didn't give a damn, that I thought controlled something, the world, or the world I wanted to inhabit, then.

In 2014, Emmie, Emilia, sometimes Emma, and I lived in that apartment in Marrickville with the neighbour who kept trying to cough the cancer out. We would come home and flip the light on and watch the cockroaches scatter.

Sometimes, we held public readings. Occasionally, privately, we shared our work. I remember sitting. All of us: writing, reading, drinking, smoking. We were poets and writers, back when we had the audacity to believe we could be such things. We were young and we were on the internet and we were in love with the written word. We had all studied, or were studying, writing and literature at university, but the books and texts we were reading seemed boring compared to the library the girls had amassed in their living room.

When I think, now, why we were so obsessed with that scene known as Alt Lit, perhaps it was because we could see ourselves in those stories, those poems. Books by Gabby Bess, Tao Lin, Sarah Jean Alexander, Jordan Castro, E.R. Kennedy, Mira Gonzalez, Sam Pink, Stacey Teague and Megan Boyle were the foundations of who we became as writers, because we felt like they understood us, were us. We were connected virtually to a group, a movement, across oceans, largely ignored, occasionally attacked, by the mainstream literary press. And because they were publishing, we thought: maybe we could do that too. It was intoxicating to think, then, in our redbrick apartment in Marrickville, that we were no different to those writers, the real writers whose books were stacked in piles on our hardwood floors.

∗∗∗

This is not an essay or a book review. This is a love story. I fell in love with writing, and then I stopped. I'm trying to figure out what happened, and whether I can fall in love again.

Here's the brief version: I wrote a lot, and failed a lot, and wrote some more, and succeeded a little, and failed a lot, and succeeded a little, and five years later, after two failed novels, two hundred thousand failed words, I emerged with two thousand words that became the opening chapters of my debut book. I wrote the rest of the book in three months, rarely stopping, barely editing, not thinking, as if high, as if the words weren't my words, as if I were merely an instrument, transcribing, but with the knowledge that if I didn't write them they – and I – would disappear.

In 2015, Scribe Publications published *Lion Attack!*

Then I suffered a ten-month-long migraine, or a tension headache, or I had a breakdown. I don't know. For ten months, the pain was constant, exacerbated by writing, reading, using computers, looking at phones or anything with a screen.

Two things happened: I became a writer who no longer wrote, and a person who could no longer communicate with the modern world. In literature, and life, I began to disappear.

There were signs. In 2013, I was sitting in my room on Canning Street trying to write a final year university essay that I had titled *If You Give Up, Fuck You* when my eyes started burning and my temples started burning and my forehead started burning. Everything went dim and everything went dull. Then I felt like I was being smashed in the back of the head by a shovel or a brick.

But I kept going.

I tried to type, closing my eyes. I tried to type,

squinting. I tried to check if the words on the document made any sense, but every time I looked at the screen the pain grew worse.

So I put on my shoes and walked to the chemist. The lady behind the counter asked how she could help and I pointed to my head. I said my head hurt and then I smiled a weird smile because I wanted to make a good impression. They'd been cracking down on codeine lately and I knew I looked shitty. But the lady just stood there with her hands on her hips. I really think I've got a migraine, I said, and then I did this little laugh. It feels like I've been hit in the head with a shovel. Then the lady's face changed. She said, Oh darling, I get them too. And then she disappeared to the backroom.

When she returned she handed me some muscle relaxants and migraine medication. She told me to take the muscle relaxants with the migraine medication and then she recommended water. She recommended hot showers. She said, I hope it goes away so you can sleep.

On the street outside the chemist I took the muscle relaxants and the migraine medications. I waited. I kept thinking about my stupid assignment. I kept thinking that it was due the next day and then I started breathing all heavy because I knew I couldn't do it and I knew how dumb it all sounded. I knew it sounded so dumb no one would ever believe it. Then I got home and lay on my bed and waited for my head to stop hurting. I looked at the ceiling and hid under the covers.

In 2014, I published *If You Give Up, Fuck You* on Facebook. It was an essay about hopes and dreams and goals and beliefs and not letting anybody fuck with your shit.

Reading the essay now feels like returning to the bedroom of my adolescence, the one I shared with my brother with the posters of Larry Bird and Michael Jordan on the wall. It makes me cringe but it also has an innocence that I wouldn't be able to recreate now. There is drive, ambition, an American enthusiasm and self-confidence that would later be confused, perhaps, rightly so, for arrogance.

I willed that motherfucker into existence, I told Sam. I wrote ten hours a day, every day. I visualized it. I saw myself holding it.

In 2014, I received a grant that allowed me to travel to the United States and Canada on a reading tour. I'd made a post on Facebook that said I would go anywhere as long as there was a bed or floor to sleep on, and someone to organize the reading. I went to Los Angeles, Portland, Oakland, Tallahassee, New Orleans, Houston, Austin, Denton, Toronto, Montreal, New York, Chicago and Minneapolis.

I met writers. I met readers.

The writers I stayed with introduced me to their friends, their writers, and we travelled in groups. We read in bookstores and warehouses and bars and apartments. We read at parties and colleges. Sometimes we read to ten people and sometimes we read to 150 people, but it felt like something, this community, this rite of passage, this pilgrimage made famous, for better or worse, by so many antipodeans before. People were hungry for words, story, literature, and before everything fell apart it seemed, briefly, that what we were doing mattered, that we were on the forefront of something, that these stories about us and the internet could cure us, or distract us, from the isolation and loneliness imposed by the newly, digitally connected world. Make no mistake, a poet said in Los Angeles at the beginning of my trip. People will study our Facebook messages and posts and G-Chat conversations for college in the future. And for a while we even believed her too.

I felt estranged from the Australian literary scene. So I looked elsewhere. I found a group of people on the internet from everywhere, including Australia, publishing and writing, and it meant something, to be included, then. We published stories on Facebook or Tumblr or we published on websites or we watched one another read on YouTube or live feeds. We chatted, gave feedback.

The scene, like all scenes, like all people, was not good or bad. It was toxic and supportive and elitist and welcoming. It was full of hate and love. The scene was an experiment. We were depressed and excited and scared and motivated. We were anxious.

Alt Lit preferred bleak narratives, those dark, sometimes humorous narratives, because they seemed relevant, or at least they seemed more real than the stories being generated by social media or traditional publishing. We were the last demographic to exist before the internet, and perhaps we were trying to make sense of that too. In his book *Lost Connections*, Johann Hari writes:

> The internet was born into a world where many people had already lost their sense of connection to each other. The collapse had already been taking place for decades by then. The web arrived offering them a kind of parody of what they were losing –Facebook friends in place of neighbors, video games in place of meaningful work, status updates in place of status in the world. The comedian Marc Maron once wrote that 'every status update is just a variation on a single request: Would someone please acknowledge me?'

To many, I think, the world seemed and still seems fractured. And for a while, in the literary sense, I suppose, for some, there was a place to fit in.

Looking back, I see the attraction, but the lifestyle – living online – further isolated the already isolated. An online community of depressed individuals who sat by themselves in bedrooms staring at computers and writing stories about the meaninglessness of life. I think, now, those pseudo-connections only made the loneliness worse. Hari writes:

Feeling lonely, it turned out, caused your cortisol levels to absolutely soar – as much as some of the most disturbing things that can ever happen to you. Becoming acutely lonely, the experiment found, was as stressful as experiencing a physical attack.

It's worth repeating – being deeply lonely seemed to cause as much stress as being punched by a stranger.

2014: Alt Lit collapsed. Several prominent members of the scene were accused of rape, statutory rape, psychological and emotional abuse. Of course, I do not, could not, know the trauma of those victims, but I watched, like many others, from computers, across states and countries in sadness, in horror; Facebook feeds and websites filled with anger and support. Dialogues appeared: on consent and respect. For a while, it seemed, we could learn. Then more were accused, and there was only despair. Facebook groups were archived. People left. The scene which had once promised so much, was now, suddenly, publicly, no different from all the others. Or perhaps it had always been this way. I just couldn't see it.

2015: I was twenty-seven, living in Sydney, earning $25,000 a year. I was between homes, staying at Toby's house and sleeping in his bed. I had a book deal. I published on Facebook. I was arrogant. I was lonely. I had few role models. I cared too much about what others thought. I prioritized writing over health, relationships and food. I became an addict to the work. There was little or no separation between the work I was publishing and myself, or the idea I had of myself. My ego grew. I became serious. I became the work, and when people commented, tweeted uncritically, negatively – that I was childish, that I was naïve, that I was a joke – I took it to heart.

I was marooned between an online community that no longer existed and a local community in which I was loved and loathed. I told myself it was good to be loved and loathed, and that I didn't need anyone, that I could go it alone. I wanted success. But I forgot to define, for myself, what success was. I see, now, that I lost my ideological reasons for writing in the first place. I told myself that if I could just get my book published then I would be accepted and money would flow, and, in doing so, I ignored the panic attacks, early headaches and sleepless nights.

These were signs. They were saying: stop writing you dumb fucking fuck. But I just wrote more.

After my book was published, I cried for days. Suddenly, the very thing I had defined myself by, the work, was no longer mine.

At the airport, flying to Melbourne for my book launch, the migraine returned, without warning, with force. I was working on a short story when my neck started hurting and my eyes started hurting and my head started hurting. And I thought this: oh no. And I thought this: not again. And I thought this: fuck. I grew dizzy. I began to sweat. I walked to the bathroom and splashed water on my face. Looked in the mirror. My eyes were bloodshot and my head veins were sticking out and I kept imagining a tiny version of myself smashing my frontal lobe.

That migraine lasted three days but I don't want to talk about the migraine. I want to talk about that sentence: I kept imagining a tiny version of myself smashing my frontal lobe. I wrote that sentence for another migraine story I published in the now defunct Australian *Rolling Stone* in 2016. The description is accurate, but it is only now that I am paying attention to the words that I hear the self-sabotage. It is only now that I am thinking about another story I wrote for *Shabby Doll House* in the middle of 2014, a ghost story, where I talk about my friend Julian, and the brain damage he suffered after a car crash, and the guilt I felt for no longer being in his life, for living in a different city, for drifting apart. In that story, Julian's character, his ghost, enters my room and says, I have accepted these truths: that dumb, meaningless things happen all the time and the world is flawed and that I am flawed too. But then his character says this, And so I ask you, Oliver: what are you afraid of? And I say, What terrifies me the most is failing or becoming incapable of doing the things I love.

The next migraine arrived one month after the airport migraine, eight months after the ghost story. It lasted ten months.

Years later, when I began to write again, I wrote small stories, no longer than a paragraph. I had forgotten how to write real stories, long stories, or was scared to, which amounts to the same thing. At some point, I told myself, literature had become boring. But that wasn't true. Literature had become terrifying, and I had become scared: of sitting, of typing, of inventing, of remembering, of trying to remember.

Here's what I remember: I remember Toby's mum was away and we were housesitting her house. There was a party. We dressed in her dresses and put coke and ketamine up our noses and boxed wine and rum and beer down our throats. Baths filled with water and people smoked and laughed and drank. Toby wore lipstick and I cried in the spare room because I wanted to wear lipstick too. I cried because I wanted my head to stop hurting and I wanted to feel normal and then I muffled my cries because I didn't want anyone to hear. I didn't want anyone to know that the migraine had returned and I didn't want Maria to know that I was blind once more. That's what we called it: my blindness. Things had been going so well lately and I didn't want to let her down. So I clenched my fists and took a breath and held it in. Then I told myself to breathe. I told myself everything would be okay and that everything was temporary and that pain was temporary too. Then I closed my eyes and said, When you open your eyes everything will be better, and it wasn't. Then I told myself that when I woke up everything would be different, and it wasn't. Then Toby came in and asked if everything was okay and I said it was even though it wasn't.

***

The next morning I let the dogs out. I watched them piss and shit on the concrete. I hosed the piss and shit from the concrete and spread it around the grass. A great smell rose from the ground and I stared at the dogs and the dogs stared back. Then the stench made a home inside me and the migraine did too. So I took three painkillers. Then I took three more. Then I started giggling – I started giggling because I couldn't feel anything any more.

But I remember other things too. I remember one afternoon I took my pain pills and Maria took her pain pills and we walked to this yoga studio down the deep end of Newtown. On the way there Maria told me she'd figured it out. You're too tense, she said. Look at you. You need to stand up straight. You need to open your shoulders. You need to breathe. So I stood up straight and opened my shoulders. I breathed. I sucked the air in and held it at the top like I knew you were meant to. Then I blew it out and emptied my lungs till there wasn't any left. Then I did it again. Then I did it again. Then I felt dizzy. Holy shit, I thought. It's working.

So we kept walking and breathing and I didn't think about the four or five or six months it had been since I'd woken up with the pain. I didn't think about how we were going to afford yoga, or what we were going to eat tomorrow, or the next day. I didn't think about the jobs I couldn't work, or the people I couldn't talk to. I didn't even picture myself jumping in front of trains. I didn't think about any of that because Maria's hand was in mine and we were breathing together.

Then she started telling me about the world and how the future was a construct and pain wasn't real. And I didn't even smile, or laugh, or tell her how bullshit it all sounded. I didn't even tell my hippy joke. I didn't say, How do you know a hippy has been to your house? They're still there. And what did they say when you told them to leave? Nah-Imma-stay. I just squeezed her hand. It was like we were different. We were a Zen couple now.

And then this happened: we walked up the stairs and handed $50 to a lady covered in tattoos. The room smelled of sage and we listened to pan flutes, then Himalayan Mountain sounds. We drank organic coconut water and stress- and adrenal-healing tea. I poured myself a cup and then I poured myself another. Then I poured myself another. Then I poured myself another. Then I swished it around my mouth, wine-tasting style. Fuck me, I said. You can really taste the healing.

And then this happened: Maria laughed and I laughed and I almost imagined us old. But then I started complaining because I was so sick of waiting. What are they . . . *making* the yoga in there? Maria told me to shut up. I told Maria how stupid it was that we always had to wait for the healing part to happen. It was like reading some dumb book for 250 pages just to figure out who survives. Maria told me to shut up again. Then she said if I shut up she'd let me sit behind her. She said I could watch her in all the bendy positions I wanted and I could be a dirty perv. She said, You'd like that wouldn't you. You dirty perv. And I told her I would. So I shut up. Then I shut up some more. Then I leant forward. I whispered, I can't wait to fuck you in your chakra. Maria whispered back, It's tight because I've kept it closed for so long. You should have seen us laughing and joking. It was almost like we were a normal couple now.

The instructor was a travelling yogi from New York City. He turned out all the lights except for a Himalayan salt lamp. He told us to lie down on our backs and then he started telling us how happy he was. He said that even though the fish were disappearing from the world's oceans and our polar ice caps were melting and our coral reefs were bleaching and a strange anomaly in the Earth's magnetic field might cause the poles to reverse in our lifetime, which would leave our atmosphere defenceless against solar winds, radiation and space debris, possibly causing an extinction event, despite that, he was happy. He said, I'm American. And we've got this guy. Maybe you've heard of him. We call him: Trump. I looked at Maria and mouthed, T R U M P? She hit me in the leg.

The instructor said, A couple days ago Trump imposed a ninety-day ban on travellers from Iran, Iraq, Libya, Somalia, Sudan, Syria and Yemen. But this morning something wonderful happened. This morning I woke up and the sun was shining and the birds were singing and I *knew* everything would be different. I could *feel* it. So I got out of bed and ate breakfast and opened the newspaper and there it was. The news! I read that a federal judge in Seattle had issued an order that blocked the President's ban. This means that refugees and travellers from those countries can travel again.

Then some people clapped and some people cheered and someone even yelled, Yewwwwwwwww. That's right! our instructor said. Yew! He told us how important it was to celebrate the little things. The small wins. And then he told us to close our eyes. He told us to start breathing our yogi breaths and he told us to let go. He said, Every time you exhale, say goodbye to your pain. So I breathed in and I breathed out and I whispered, *Goodbye pain. Goodbye.*

I said goodbye to the nights Maria twisted and turned and yelled in her sleep and to the mornings I lay awake next to her. I'd try to wake her but I couldn't. And I just wanted her to wake. I wanted to tell her that everything would be okay, and then I said: You're okay. You're okay, because I'd seen enough movies to know if you repeated something then it would come true.

So say this with me now. Say: You're okay. You're okay. And maybe it will come true.

Then I thought about the migraine and the world and how nothing made sense.

I thought how the doctors didn't know and the optometrists didn't know and the psychologists didn't know and then I thought how the world was one big fucking: I don't know.

I thought how Trump was a president. Then I thought how reality TV stars could become leaders and leaders could become lords. I knew people could change. So I said a prayer not to God but to Trump. I prayed: if you let me get better and you let Maria get better I'll do anything. I swear. I promise. Amen.

So then the instructor began chanting his chants, and we chanted too. We chanted like we believed. We chanted like we belonged. We were a bunch of strangers chanting phrases from a language we didn't speak and a religion we didn't understand and this was called: healing.

Then the instructor told us to open our eyes, and I opened my eyes and it was like the world was different now. Maria wasn't twisting or turning or yelling, and I wasn't crying or clenching or smashing my head into a wall. It was like the past had never happened and the voices inside our heads were new voices. And they were whispering their new whispers too. And they weren't being mean or nasty or calling us pieces of shit. These were the new voices that said: you can make this world anything you want. Even a kind world. You just have to believe.

But then something happened and I swear this is true. The window went *BANG*. And the window cracked. Then we went to the window and found a bird bleeding on the pavement below. Its wings were broken and its back was broken and it kept trying to fly. It kept flapping its broken wings but instead of flying it just made jerky snow angels in the grass and glass.

So then we returned to our mats and the class went on and I kept waiting for the instructor to say something. I kept waiting for him to explain that sometimes the world tries to break you. I kept waiting for him to tell us that no matter what we couldn't give up. But he didn't. He just told everyone to downward dog. And everyone obeyed. And everyone pretended the window wasn't broken, and a bird wasn't dying, and the world was still the world from a few minutes ago.

Everyone pretended their partners loved them, and their parents were proud of them, and when Maria and I returned home we took our pain pills and we went on pretending too. We drew a bath and we lit candles and we drank wine and we giggled and we didn't talk about the cuts appearing on Maria's thighs or how she'd begun locking herself in the bathroom at night. We didn't talk about how the migraine had started talking to me: You will not get better. No one can help you. Soon, it will be your turn too. And that night as I lay in bed I started laughing because I knew all you had to do was lie. I knew if you could believe in lies you could believe in anything. I knew if you did it enough then those lies would become true.

So now I write this book and I fill it with lies. Maria never left. The window never smashed. The bird never died. And if you read on you become part of the lie too. So say this with me now. Say: You're okay. You're okay. And maybe it will come true.

Did it work?

Listen: there are times when I don't remember much, but occasionally I close my eyes and I see everything. I see it all.

Ten months later Mum flew to Sydney and we spent an afternoon drinking at the Lord Wolseley Hotel. I didn't ask why she came. I didn't have to. She'd heard my voice on the phone.

She asked if I wanted to talk about earlier that day when she found me crying in the bathroom and then she told me I could tell her anything. She told me shutting down was the easy thing, but the brave thing was to talk. She said I could cry if I wanted and it wouldn't matter. It wouldn't matter that a twenty-seven-year-old boy was at the pub crying with his mum.

So I breathed and I breathed and then I began to cry. I cried and people laughed and I told her I felt alone. I told her I felt scared and I wondered if she'd felt that? Then she said, Breathe, Oliver. Breathe, and I knew she had too. I tried to explain the pain in my head and I couldn't, and I tried to imagine what I would do when I got home and I couldn't, and then I buried my face in my hands and whispered, I just wish it would all go away. Mum squeezed my hand and told me she loved me. She told me she cared. I squeezed back. She said, I'll always be there for you. You know that, right? and I told her I knew.

And then I was five again, and I'd fallen off my bike, and Mum was asking me where it hurt. I'd ridden my bike into the railing that overlooks Lake Burley Griffin, and I pointed at my knees. I was bleeding, a mess, one training wheel bent 45 degrees in the wrong direction, and Mum kept asking strangers if they could help us. Can you help us? Can you help us? Can you help us? Can you? Then a bodybuilder bent my training wheels back and I couldn't believe my bike was perfect again. I couldn't believe magicians were real and knees could stop bleeding. I couldn't believe all the bad things could go away: you just had to ask.

And then I was twenty-seven again, and my arms were reaching around my mother and I was crying into her shirt. I told her I couldn't do it any more. I needed her. I needed help. I said, Please, please, and my voice went all high and I said, I just . . . don't know what to do. Mum held me. Told me I wasn't alone. I held her tighter. I took two painkillers and they mixed with the alcohol and the six painkillers I'd taken before. I told her I was sorry. I wished she didn't have to see. Mum kept saying, It's okay, it's okay. But I knew it wasn't. She was sobbing, and I knew we were both in pain now. I knew the world was bullshit because there was pain inside all of us, even our mothers. So we sat there and I smoked another cigarette and drank another beer. Then I drank another beer. Then I drank another beer. Then I drank one more.

Then I began to laugh because it was almost like the pain was gone now. I began to laugh because we lived in a stupid world where all you had to do was put the terrible things inside you to feel good again once more. I laughed and I laughed because everyone was staring at screens and no one could see that the whole world was changing. No one could see the guy at the table beside us who woke in the middle of the night just to check Tinder, just to check Messenger, just to check if someone cared. And no one could see the girl who checked her messages every five minutes because the person she'd fucked had seen her message but hadn't written back. And no one could see me either. No one could see me because I was invisible, and I laughed because the world was telling a new story now, and no one knew what it was.

***

Gerald Murnane in conversation with Sean O'Beirne at the Wheeler Centre: 'The feeling when you are struck down by tragedy, and there would be many people here listening who have had that happen to them, the feeling is that you are sort of singled out and separate, that other people would never understand the thing you have been through.'

To what end do the fictions of our mind dictate our behaviours, our thoughts and feelings, our perceptions of the world we understand to be true? It sounds obvious, now, to answer: a great deal, but at the time, during those ten months, I had no idea. The mechanisms through which I created – blindly, playfully – had broken and in the place of creation there was only fear: of judgement, of rejection, which now, I tell myself, manifested as pain. But maybe that's all bullshit too. Perhaps our bodies just weren't designed to spend ten hours at a time in sedentary positions undertaking repetitive tasks. Perhaps I was weak, as an optometrist told me, smiling, when he explained I had blown out my eyes, the visual system that allowed me to focus, to make sense of all the things in front of me that I could no longer see. I remember, each morning, sitting with a piece of string that I held in front of my nose. There were two beads, one close and one far away, and my eyes would jump from one to the other, training them, again, to converge.

I told you this was a love story.

But this is a trust story.

I'm learning how to trust my body again, to sit, to write. I'm learning how to trust my mind to believe that the worlds that exist in my head can exist on the page too.

I like to think that I'm resilient, strong. I'm certainly stubborn. I like to think that I'm tough. But I also have to reconcile with the fact that something happened: a ten-month-long migraine? A breakdown? My body shut down.

I remember leaving Sydney, returning to Brisbane, to my parents' house. On that first night I asked my dad if it was going to get better. Of course it will, he said. But for now let's not worry about that. Let's decide what we are going to have for dinner.

I suppose we write to make sense of the pain, not to add to it. But after the migraine went away, I still found it more or less impossible to sit, to type. I had to learn how to sit in chairs again, how to look at computers, books, at phones. Sitting at a computer, the act of writing, had caused the pain to begin with, at least in my head, and for many years after the migraine dissipated I still felt an extreme anxiety whenever I sat, or tried to sit, in front of the computer or laptop. Even the thought of writing or typing, on a phone or laptop or the page, when I wondered about the future, whether I would be able to message friends, work a job, look up a train time-table, would trigger a relapse and the pain would return. I would begin to sweat. Shake. It's not going to be like last time, Mum would say. And then she'd tell me to repeat it. It's not going to be like last time. It's not going to be like last time. Sometimes, even now, the pain returns. But I just tell myself to breathe. I lie down. Meditate. And then I remind myself, again, that it won't be like last time. I remind myself that the stories we tell ourselves are the ones that become true.

Scott McClanahan: 'The only hope we have are our bodies. We're all trapped in them and we all hate them, and it's this reason why we're comic and not tragic.'

***

These days, I'm a slow writer. I listen to my body. I take breaks. I write with a pencil, in fragments, between stations, while working on the train. With the pen we became adolescents and with the computer, fully grown. But with the pencil we become children again.

On my 28th birthday, shortly before leaving Brisbane and returning to Sydney, Dad gave me a copy of *The Adventures of Tintin: The Secret of the Unicorn*. Inside the cover, he wrote the following inscription, and with his permission, I would like to close this story and leave it with you.

Dear Oliver,

Some of my fondest memories of you as a little boy centred on our time together reading Tintin, *with you on my lap, asking me to repeat my Captain Haddock rants, and all his colourful language. We made our way through many Tintin stories together, and on reflection, I think they were not only a great bonding time, but great therapy for me.*

And now, years later, it occurs to me that they may be great therapy for you too. It is truly wonderful to escape into these adventures, pushing today's worries to the background, and simply enjoying these creative and colourful characters. I hope they bring out the little boy in you again.

Love Dad

Angels

One morning I was sent to Lidcombe to pick up a train, and on the way there this guy in a mid-riff top started telling me how he used to convert pushbikes into motorbikes. Used to convert 'em, he said. Guess what I did after? Rode 'em down Parramatta Road. Then he put his hands on an imaginary motorbike, twisted one wrist back and forth and started making engine noises. REOW, REOW, he said, revving. Little cunt would go *put, put, put*. Then I'd drop the clutch. REOW, REOW – see ya's later! Then he grinned and started yelling, YEAH, SEE YA'S LATER, COPPAAAAAAAS! They'd tell me to slow down and I'd say, What? like I couldn't hear 'em. Then I'd take my hand off the accelerator and give them the bird. Then he pretended the window was a cop and he gave it the bird. Naa, he said. It was good fun. At least, till Sue died.

He started shifting in his seat, then, and telling me how he told her to stop drinking. I told her to stop. But did she listen? I told her I'd seen me dad die, seen me brother die, and now I was gonna watch her die too. But she didn't listen. And then she was in hospital and her oesophagus started filling with blood. They drained it.

It filled up again. They drained it. It filled up again. Then she died. Fuck, I said. I'm sorry. Not your fault, he said, looking at the ceiling. I guess that's just how it goes. But I miss her, you know?

We sat for a while, and I asked if she ever visited him. Yeah, he said. Every time I want to drink. I see her almost every day.

In some ways I used to think I had a guardian angel too. During my time in Brisbane, my mother and I would go for walks and talk about life and love and pain and family, and one afternoon, on the way to Mount Coot-tha, we spoke about her mother, my grandmother, who we couldn't call Grandma, but Hazo, and how she was dying.

Mum told it like this: on her deathbed, in the hospital, she lay with her children by her side. There was Mum and Auntie Jo and Uncle Steve and Uncle Tim. There was Minnie too. Minnie was her dog, this Maltese Poodle cross that, in its later years, developed a smoker's cough, and whose fur was no longer white but stained nicotine yellow.

They flew in from different parts of Australia – Perth, Brisbane, Gosford. And they were smiling but they were sad. They knew she was dying. So they went in with flowers and tried not to cry. But Hazo told them to stop being miserable. Good God, she said, and dismissed them with her hand. She told them everything had been taken care of and that there was no need for a funeral. She was donating her body to science. That was that. Her body would be returned ten years later and they could scatter her ashes over the plants in the botanical gardens. She asked to see Minnie, so Jo tried passing Minnie to Hazo but Minnie began to squirm. She twisted and she shook and then she jumped from Jo's arms and ran out the door. But Hazo just smiled. She began nodding. She said, Minnie knows. Minnie knows. And the way she repeated it, I don't know, made it true.

But if you really knew her, you called her Haze. Why? Maybe this: She started smoking when she was twelve. She smoked and she smoked and she quit when she was dead. One summer when her son Tim was fourteen he started smoking too. Horrible things, Haze said. Nasty. They'll kill you. But Tim kept right on smoking. Smoke. Smoke. One day Haze said, I'll give you $500 a month if you quit. So Tim quit and he was rich but Haze was losing too much money. Tim told Haze she could stop the payments if she quit too. So she did. One day passed. Two days. On the third day Tim came home from school and there was Haze, lighting up. Puff. Puff. Hey Mum,

Tim said. But Haze just told him she didn't want to hear it. Life's boring, she said. What's the point? There's nothing else to do.

But Haze was more than her cigarettes. She loved gambling too. In the evenings she'd ask her kids who was feeling lucky. You feeling lucky, Vick? How 'bout you, Tim? Steve? Jo? Course those were the days when kids were still allowed in the RSLs to help their mothers play the pokies while they learned about the world. And so they went. They played the machines, Haze supervising, five at a time. You sure you're feeling lucky, Vick? Nope? Then you can take yourself home. She showed them how to rub the machines, how to feed them. Come on, she'd say. You gotta *know* them. You gotta *believe*. Then their faces would light up because Haze was the one who made the machines sing.

One summer Haze took them to Bundanoon. They stayed at this campground. There was a fancy dress party and there were prizes for the most creatively dressed kid. Everyone was five and Tim was twelve. He was small, sort of sensitive about it, and just wanted to fit in. All the other kids were dressed as princes and princesses and werewolves and rugby players. But Haze thought their costumes were rubbish. Not creative at all, she said. So she went out and found a branch. Hold it, she said. Look, you're a bonsai.

Mum told me those stories, then, as we walked through Mount Coot-tha. We laughed together and spoke about the dead. She told me Haze never swore. She rarely drank. She was a tough woman. A strong woman. She told me when Haze turned fifty she had all her teeth removed and replaced with a set of dentures.

But then she told me something else. She told me there wasn't a lot of warmth. I just want to make sure you're okay, she said. And I smiled and told her I was fine. That I was getting better. I'm crying less and the migraines are gone, mostly. I told her I no longer wanted to die.

Then it was sundown and we were beneath the large eucalypts on a fire trail trying to find the path, those small offshoots, that would take us back towards the car. I told her my favourite memory of Haze, the one that stood out, was this:

Haze was sixty-something, ten years younger, and hooked up to her ventilator, though she called it The Machine. She'd just installed Foxtel to watch boxing on the television, and she was watching it. It was Christmas Eve and we were sitting around the Christmas tree, guessing at presents. I bet it's a book, my cousin said. Maybe it's a Nintendo. I hope it's a Nintendo. Books can get stuffed. This advertisement came on for patches or Nicorette gum, something for quitting cigarettes, and Haze said, Good God. Then she turned to us under the Christmas tree and told us how stupid it all was. How ridiculous. Blow 'em! she said, and then she got up, unplugged herself from The Machine and walked towards the door. She had a different dog then, I forget its name, but she picked it up and went outside. She smoked. One cigarette. Two cigarettes. Three cigarettes. She smoked and I remember the way she smiled. She smoked like she'd won. And then, I told Mum, something happened. I saw something. I told her the smoke above her head had formed a ring – neatly, perfectly – and I thought she was an angel. I thought she was an angel who smoked and watched boxing and that she'd teach me how to be strong. I came from her blood and I thought that meant something. I thought she'd watch over me. I thought—

We were going to get married, the guy in the mid-riff said, after a while. Or I think we were. I was gonna ask her, but then. He hesitated for a second. I don't know. I just want to say thanks, you know, for talking. Not many people wanna talk these days. I ride the train all day and try to talk to people, but no one ever really talks. It gets lonely, he said, laughing. But naa, it's okay. I mean, I'm okay. It's my pleasure, I said.

We were arriving at Lidcombe, then, and we both stood. I just wish people knew how beautiful she was. How kind. Every morning she'd fly into the room with her arms outstretched like an airplane and say, Get the fuck outta bed!, crashing into me. She'd call me her twin towers 'cause of my muscles, he said, grinning, flexing. We'd smoke cigarettes and drink coffee together. I just . . . I miss that. I miss her. He held out his hand, then, and I shook it, and after that I watched him walk away, and he looked so pathetic and beautiful and fucked up and heart-broken, and I felt like I knew him because he reminded me of me.

Literature

In those first few days of what I will call Freedom, or almost Freedom, I kept waking at odd hours of the morning, in cold sweats, from dreams in which I was the protagonist and the migraine had returned. What was most terrifying, then, I think, was not that the pain had returned – although that was, certainly, terrifying – but that my ability to read, to pass the time in a way that didn't involve crying or staring at a ceiling, would suddenly, absurdly, be removed once more. I guess what I am trying to say is that I was terrified, again, of being alone.

We're going to make a plan, Mum said, as we drove through Milton towards the Indooroopilly library, and so we spoke about the psychologists I would see, and the hikes we would complete, and the yoga classes we would do, all the time listening to Phillip Glass or Ludovico Einaudi, as if we were in our own movie, this movie about mothers and sons, hope and pain—I love this shithole, I said, as we passed the XXXX brewery, and then Mum looked at me in the mirror and said, I've missed that. What? That smile.

It's hard to describe how I felt walking through the Indooroopilly shopping centre, no longer an adolescent – that shopping centre where we used to attend movie marathons, McDonald's Coke cups filled to the brim with Bundaberg Rum, that movie theatre where I had my first kiss, where I celebrated, silently, and later, like a loser, yelling YES, punching my fist to the sky – but as a man, or a boy pretending to be a man, who had moved back in with his parents, but if I had to try, really try, the best I could say was that I was terrified, and shaking.

I remember, entering the library, I slowed: reading or trying to read had given me the headache or pain to begin with, and I saw the books not as books, but as bombs or poison or as reminders – of my own book and my own perceived failings, of the texts I had tried to read, thought I could read, but could then not read, plunged, once more, into my own head, into isolation, into pain. It'll be okay, Mum said. Just take it slow. And so we walked, together, under those bright lights, breathing, hoping, and I made one of those ridiculous deals we made as children: where we prayed to God or the sky or ourselves and promised to behave, to be better, if we could just be normal; if everything could be okay.

If this all seems ludicrous it's only because it was, and as I walked around the aisles I closed my eyes the way I used to when I worked at the Sydney Opera House, when I pretended to check all those tickets, knowing that if I read those tiny letters the migraine would outstrip the codeine and I would be unable to pretend nothing hurt. And so, I walked blindly, approximately, to where the C section was and selected Luke Carman's *An Elegant Young Man*, and then to the M section, and selected Loorie Moore's *Bark,* and then to the O section, and selected Tim O'Brien's *The Things They Carried.* On the car trip home, I glanced briefly, indulgently, at the covers and tried to remember the thrill of reading books as a child.

That evening I lay on my back, in the room where I had spent my adolescence, and I pressed my neck into the carpet, trying to straighten it, trying to keep the door open to the house, the muscles, where the headaches lived, the way the Healer had shown me I should. And then, I remember, I groped for one of the books by my side. When it came into vision, I read *The Things They Carried,* and I held that book, arms straight, high above my head, glancing at it, then looking away, then glancing again, as if it were Medusa, as if it had the power to return me to that private hell, something inescapable, to stone. The reading was slow, and rather than words I focused on my breath, keeping it even, measured. After each paragraph, I would put the book down and say: You're okay. Reading is okay. And every paragraph the pain didn't return was another paragraph closer to making that true.

Around this time, absurdly, I bought a brown notebook and titled it *Notes For Book*. I still couldn't write, could barely read, but I told myself that one day I would write all about the migraine and Maria and that no one would ever see those notes, and that I could write whatever I wanted. I told myself I was going to make mistakes and I wasn't going to think and I was going to tell the whole story once and for all. The most important part, I knew, was to make it unsentimental – throw in all the heavy stuff, sure, but pepper it with all the beautiful and funny parts that happened too. A real story from a real author. Something for those literary magazines I no longer read and had stopped submitting to long ago.

For years, I failed miserably. It wasn't a question of discipline, but proximity. I felt too close to the work. I needed something, a buffer, distance, space where we could roam not as people but characters, for that was what we were, then, at least in my mind anyway: characters, distortions of memory, ghosts.

On the train, on the backs of old train diagrams, I tried adding chapters, then deleting them; eventually, I tried changing the protagonist. At first it seemed repulsive, and I recalled with some humour a creative writing teacher from years earlier who had said, Never, *never* change the protagonist midway through a narrative. It's confusing, jarring. It's too *jarring*, he repeated, and then, suddenly, began commenting on the short story, and how it was dead. We all laughed nervously and began making mental notes to return to that scarcely more profitable model, the novel, while many of us, for various reasons, stopped writing all together. However, what stands out for me now, beyond that wonderful repetition, was the pace at which he repeated the word *jarring*, as if it were something awful, something to skip over, something to omit. Perhaps that's why I find comfort in the essay: because they can be jarring; because sometimes from the wreckage the wounded crawl, they stand up, they sing.

Jep Jep

Her name was Jessie, or Jep, or Jep Jep, or Jeplestein, though certainly not Tinsel, her name before we picked her up shortly after moving to Texas, before Y2K, when people were stockpiling water, canned goods and guns at Walmart, preparing for the end. Jep Jep, as we mostly called her, was a mother, a Husky x Australian Shepherd, or an American Eskimo x wolf who had been abused and abandoned and forgotten to the RSPCA. One afternoon my mum and sister were walking through the mall when they saw her in a shop window. My father, then, was vehemently against getting a dog, but the way she cowered in the corner, pleading, almost begging, not the way most dogs do – energetically, with their paws, their necks, their heads – but with her legs crossed, elegantly, with her eyes downcast – it was too much. So they did a lap of the mall, discussed the matter and before they passed, again, that horrific Abercrombie & Fitch store, returned, reasoning that they couldn't just leave her, that Dad would understand, or would grow to understand, or would, perhaps, even grow to love her too. But when they arrived, she was gone. My sister was eight, heartbroken. She burst into tears, and they left assuming the worst: that someone else had picked her up, that she was gone, that she was never coming back. I just hope she didn't get picked up by some arsehole, she said, a word she'd learned from my father, who, famously, loved to call strangers arseholes, and my mother didn't even correct her because she hoped it was true too.

The following week, however, my father and sister returned; Dad was trying to find a tie with a sailing ship on it, but then my sister sprinted into the store. DAD, she screamed. DADDD! TINSEL'S BACK! Who the hell's Tinsel? Dad asked, or I like to think he asked, now, because it's funny, and because he was always asking who the hell certain people were – like the time, years later, we were in the car listening to the radio announce that Flume had won a Grammy and Dad turned around and said, And who the hell's PHLEGM? – but in the end my sister said they couldn't leave her, not again, and so they called Mum and made a deal: we can bring her home, Dad said, but she's not my responsibility. I don't have time to feed or train her, that's up to the rest of you. And so Tinsel came home in the back of our minivan, cowering in the corner of her straw-filled crate, occasionally whimpering, though mostly keeping quiet – the way she knew it was safe; the way she'd been taught her entire life.

What the hell kind of name is Tinsel anyway? Dad said. What is she, an ornament? Something cheap and flashy? No thank you. And so, in principle, Tinsel became Jessie, though in reality she struggled to forget her old name, her old life. Around men: my father, the postman, our neighbours, she would almost squat, her tail between her legs, as if she had been struck, or almost struck, or was replaying the memory of being struck long ago. Course I was ten or eleven then, and my brother was perhaps seven, and mostly she would bound up to us: her whole body shaking, wagging, playing – but there were other times when she would pause, as if remembering what we were capable of, or what we could become.

The details are shaky, though with a little research we learned she'd been abused. Her owner beat her for years, and after she finally whelped six puppies, he abandoned her on the street. During those first weeks, months, she didn't bark, and we wondered, for a time, if she even knew how. It's okay, we'd say, or my father would say, bringing her fresh water and food while she retreated, gazing up at him from the grass, this mother who looked like a wolf or a raccoon – and then, when he was far enough away, she would nudge forward, pausing, before nudging forward again, unsure of the water and food and this new emotion, this strange man who seemed to suggest that the world could be kind.

Right, Dad said. She gets three walks a day. So get your barge-arses moving – she's a sled dog! Get on your bikes and take her for a ride. And so we rode, around and around that awful suburb called Hayden's Run, around suburbia, with all those American flags, huge and crass like the people, spilling on to the lawns of houses, and Jep Jep would run beside us, usually ahead of us, though occasionally behind us, only to stop, suddenly, as if she had forgotten, or remembered, who she was. What I remember most is not our bloody knees or shins or elbows, but the way her eyes would roll to the back of her head, how her back would twist and her head would tremor and how her tail would spasm – and then how she would pause. I like to think of these moments, now, because they appear frozen in time, a comma before the crisis, when we were young and Jep Jep was alive, before we would inevitably fall and Jep Jep would go what we called 'Full Psycho', sprinting into the bushes, into brush, running, running, from herself, her past, anywhere, away – but perhaps that is all a fiction; perhaps she was running towards something too, and these glitches were not glitches but celebrations, uncontrollable expressions from deep inside that she was finally free.

Did you ever have dogs growing up? I asked Dad, one afternoon, but he said, No, that he had never had dogs, that his parents hadn't been interested in dogs, that, instead, in Canada, they had had cats, one or two of which, during the winter and seeking warmth, had crawled into the family's car engine and died. Mum, on the other hand, had had several dogs. The first was called Porcia, named after the wife of an obscure politician from the late Roman Republic who took a leading role in the assassination of Julius Caesar. The second dog was called Gurly, an old, beautiful dog who was run over on Christmas Eve. The third dog was called Lucy who may or may not have drowned. The fourth dog was called Manfred, a miniature Collie who had hip surgery and lived a long and prosperous life. The fifth was called Toby, a Labrador cross that Mum brought home from the market, who chewed all her father's socks and ripped sheets off the line and who, after Mum left home, was donated to a posh neighbour and lived like a prince. Then there was Jojo, Mum's sixth dog and our family's first, who spent all her time digging holes and escaping, running the streets of Canberra, hanging out at Erindale shops – when we left we gave her to a friend, and not much changed because it was almost like she'd never been ours at all. The next, the last, was Jessie, Jess, Jep Jep, Jep.

In that first year she barely came into the kitchen, preferring to stay in her crate, in the laundry. Jep Jep! we would say. Come on! Come on, girl! But she would not come; the laundry was hers; she knew that space, though I wonder, now, if it was more than that, something as grand and simple as not recognizing her new name.

But if I could only tell you about her hearing, how she heard Dad coming home long before anybody else, before his car reached our street, how her head would raise and her tail would wag and how she would sprint from one side of the yard to the other, not caring, for a moment, about the squirrels or other dogs roaming their yards, and how she whimpered and how she barked – how, eventually, she remembered how to bark. If I could only tell you about her paws, how she placed them, one over the other, like a lady, as my mother would say, at first, breaching the threshold between the laundry and the kitchen, and then, slowly, one evening, moving, cautiously, into the kitchen, her paws silent as she came to a rest, not with us but close to us, away from the table. I was, maybe, twelve then, and after dinner I would practise jumping exercises in our garage from a program called Air Alert 2. It was hot during those Texan nights and I would spend them, determinedly, alone, jumping, trying to increase my vertical, to change, to make basketball A team, to be stronger, better, to fit in, whatever that meant. Sometimes, Jep Jep would sit with me, panting on the concrete, though usually I would find her afterwards, sitting, facing Mum and Dad in the living room – her paws now millimetres from the kitchen hardwood–living room carpet divide. I remember some-times we would pick her up and hold her on her back as if she was a newborn, taking her from the kitchen to the living room, and sometimes, if we made it that far, even upstairs. But mostly she would whimper and squirm, sometimes even escaping and sprinting back to the laun-dry, wetting herself, as if remembering some terrible thing that none of us could know.

It's almost as if this were a eulogy, I think now, and per-haps it is.

One summer we took her to Gardener Falls, this national park several hours outside of Houston with campgrounds and a river and those trees you could jump out of into that murky brown water. Jep Jep wasn't an ocean girl, the waves scared her, but that summer she followed us down to the river. My sister jumped out of the highest tree first; my brother and I followed, and then, splashing and laughing, we called Jep Jep to join. At first, she sniffed the water. She paced. But then, from the bank, she jumped. The river was wide, maybe 60 metres across, and she swam to us, around us; we were standing in the shallows, then, and she rounded us up as if we were her sheep, head above the water, her nose sniffing little sniffs, before returning to the bank. Then, perhaps a minute later, she jumped into the river again, this time swimming farther, past where we had been, perhaps a quarter of the way across before looping to the shore once more. On her third trip, she swam all the way to the middle, and we cheered; this dog who had now taken the form of a tugboat, or a beautiful drowned rat, U-turning in that river, panting and paddling through the water that reflected like quartz in that afternoon sun. For a while, she relaxed, breathing, staring out across the river. By now, we were packing up; the sun was fading, but then, as Dad put away the last of the chairs, she leapt into the river for a final time, and we watched her swim clear to the other side. On her way back, we cheered, hollered. We yelled, Go Jepppp! Wooohooooo! Come home! And I swear to God when she returned she looked different, like a mother who had never lost her children – or a mother who had – daring to trust again, to believe that she might be okay, that she might not be alone.

Well, we can't leave her here, Dad said, as we folded our sausages into bread, Jep Jep munching her own saus-ages that we fed her, in secret, during dinner on the kitchen floor. Dad had been made redundant; we were to go to Hong Kong, or return home, and the idea that we might leave had seemed impossible until then, though, in truth, it was something I'd prayed for. I was fourteen and I didn't understand America and I didn't understand myself. Sometimes, in the evenings, I would lie on the laundry floor, my head on Jep Jep's back, thinking about all the things that were wrong with me even though I didn't know why. Why are people mean? Why are they cruel? Where are my real friends? When will I get hair under my arms? When will my dick grow? I just want to grow. I'm alone. But Jep Jep would just lie there, breathing, taking my weight – this mother who knew, instinctively, that the trick was just to keep breathing.

So we returned to Brisbane, to that house my mother ran as a Bed & Breakfast on Kelvin Grove Road, where Jep Jep lived mainly in the backyard under the stairs, and in the summer we would get her shaved, and she would return changed, as if a child, a puppy, frisky, and with a pink bow in her hair. Sometimes, when I picture her now, all I see is her naughty face and that pink bow: lopsided and filthy from chasing those fucking arsehole possums around the yard. What's that, Jess? Dad would say as the possums hissed their devil hisses and her ears pricked up and she prepared, as she had always done, to go 'Full Psycho'. Fucking arsehole possums! Get them, Jess! Dad would say, and then Jess would be off, sprinting, clearing, or almost clearing, the eleven stairs from the deck to the backyard, and the possums would flee, and Dad would tell another story about how heroic she was, saving Mum's flowers, those basil plants and parsley plants and pansies and dwarf snapdragons and bamboo and all the other plants and trees that lined our backyard, that familiar space within the Bed & Breakfast that, even though it was communal, Mum had made very much our own.

I remember, a year or two after high school, I travelled overseas, and Nadia would walk Jessie around Kelvin Grove, Red Hill, Paddington, listening to The Shins or Elliott Smith or Rufus Wainwright's 'Cigarettes and Chocolate Milk', and that when I returned she said that I'd gotten bigger, that I'd filled out, and that when she walked Jessie around the block lots of guys would stare, but she wouldn't notice, or barely notice, too busy lusting over the idea of having her own dog that she could walk after school. And I remember the New Year's my parents were away and Toby, Ben and Jack flew from Sydney to Brisbane and we went to a party and got high and separated and in the morning Toby and Jack, drinking whisky and eating tramadol, shoplifted dog shampoo, conditioner and treats from Coles and when I returned to our house, my parents' sanctuary, three chairs were broken and Toby had put our trampoline in the pool and was sitting on it, grinning, because he'd washed Jep Jep eight times and she no longer smelled and he yelled, I even fed her too! And I remember the night it hailed and the hail banked up and Brisbane turned white and we took Jep Jep and some old skate decks to the golf course and Jep Jep rolled around in the slush that we pretended was snow and we used the skate decks as snowboards and put Jep Jep on the skate deck and watched her ride down the hills.

It's hard to know how old Jep Jep really was. At some point, we stopped counting – but one evening she fell down the stairs. By now, my sister and I had finished school, though perhaps my brother had too; we were eating on the deck when we heard a thud, then a thud, then a thud and then nothing. Dad was the first to get up, and we sat there, at first, confused, and then, in a sort of paralysis, staring at one another as we heard Dad say, It's okay, Jess. Come here, girl. Everything will be okay. Her back legs had been going for a while – occasionally, accidentally, she'd sit mid-stride, other times she'd drag her paws along the ground, sometimes she would simply urinate where she sat as if she were an old lady, a grandma or a great-grandma riddled with arthritis just trying to make it to the bathroom, which, in fact, she was. Dad kept saying, There, there, as he picked her up and carried her to the garden to pee. That's a good girl. And I still remember them emerging from the stairs: Dad holding her like a newborn, then placing her down, fetching her water, a piece of chicken, a treat, running a brush, gently, through her coat, her hair that had begun to patch and bald, this wolf of a dog who had begun to resemble, now, an elderly raccoon, who, even in the weeks after, even when she couldn't, would still attempt to scale the stairs when we, though especially my father, got home.

And so my father went about rigging up some wheels. He went into the shed and sketched some prototypes and conceived a harness and drove to Bunnings to find the wood and bearings and all the materials required to make Jep Jep mobile again. But that weekend, as Dad was putting the final touches on what we called 'The Rig', my sister asked if she could take Jep Jep to the country. Someone was having a party. There would be new smells, people, a bonfire. Just make sure you take care of her, Dad said, with the same tone he always used when expressing, or trying to express, his feelings, or the things he couldn't live without. And so, that weekend, she drove, Jep Jep on the back seat, listening to old tapes: Bob Dylan, Leonard Cohen, Creedence Clearwater Revival, the city becoming suburbia, then grass and trees, then plains and more plains. After they arrived, Brigitte helped her out of the car, and she sniffed the earth, the plants – a bonfire grew and Brigitte carried her towards that too. People drank Bundaberg Rum and XXXX and spoke about their lives or made jokes or pretended to be different or remembered their lives from long ago. Jep Jep licked the ground and stared at the fire; people patted her patchy coat and she smelled their smells, and then the wind brought even new smells too. And then, Brigitte said, maybe an hour later, she saw something she couldn't believe. Jep Jep's ears had pricked up and she was standing and her head and neck had arched a straight arrow towards the moon. And suddenly, she didn't look fifteen or sixteen or seventeen, but a puppy; she let out a howl; her eyes rolled, and she ran.

And so her legs worked, again, and continued working during those final years, that time period where she, absurdly, had begun approaching us not from the front, but the rear, when she would back into us in a sort of grinding motion, wiggling her bottom against our legs, doing whatever she wanted, the way people, though especially the elderly, do after they stop caring about what other people think. But this too was a period of cheese, lots of cheese; in the evenings she no longer ate kibble or canned food, she was beyond that now, and so she ate what we ate: chicken, spaghetti, sausages, but, like my grandfather, who was ninety-four, and who would sneak downstairs in his own home in Canberra to down packets of sugar and nibble on cheese blocks from the fridge, it was the cheese, I'm sure, that my father fed her that kept her living so long. How old was she? It's hard to know. At times, she was eighteen, at others, twenty-one, but after a certain point, I just told people she was twenty. Oh my God, look at her! students, though generally girls, from QUT would say as my mother and I walked her slowly around the campus. Inevitably, they would crouch to pet her, and we would tell them to approach from the front, to let her sniff their hand, not because she was aggressive, but because, at the age of twenty, she had become deaf and blind.

In a sense, I had returned home that summer because I was blind too. I was twenty-seven and had suffered a ten-month migraine that left me dependent, or mostly dependent, on others, unable to look at books, a phone or a computer, the things up close, anything with a screen, and in those early months of 2016 I would lie, once more, on the floor next to Jep, our beautiful girl, both of us, suddenly, no longer adults, but helpless, children. Dad would keep track of Jep's deworming schedule, hiding, when necessary, those pills she hated in her chicken, her treats, while Mum read to me from Elizabeth Gilbert's *Big Magic*, that book I loved, not because of the content – I was, pathetically, too proud for that – but because it was the first book I had *heard* in as long as I could remember. The pain, then, was sporadic, occasionally horrific, but during that first recovery what I remember most is Jep Jep and how my father washed her and held her and rubbed cream into her bald, rashed skin; I remember the car trips that Mum and I went on to Mount Coot-tha, Jep Jep in the back, and how we spoke about pain: what to do with it, how to treat it, as she said, like a friend. At the time, that phrase angered me, seemed inconceivable, but now, nearly six years on, I think, maybe, I am beginning to understand. Without that pain I wouldn't have had *this* story; I wouldn't have returned to Brisbane; I wouldn't have been able to spend those last months with Jep, my family; I wouldn't have been able to say goodbye.

Her last meal was spaghetti. I had returned to Sydney, attempting to resume a life, a writing life, I was no longer sure I wanted, when I got the call. We were on speaker-phone, and Mum and Dad told me that her kidneys had started failing, that she had been put on painkillers, that she had stopped barking, that once again she could barely walk. At the vet, they draped her in a green blanket and my parents held on to her back, her paws. And so she went, I heard, like she came: quietly, but also differently: peacefully, and, I think, I hope, no longer alone. And if this really were a eulogy I would wish only to conclude like this: that she was a girl who had known suffering, true suffering, but that miracles were still possible, that our bodies could fail and start working again – she had proven, at least to me, that it might be possible to start over, to feel okay, to learn to love and trust, uncompromisingly and wholeheartedly, again.

Work

A few years after the migraine I flew to Rome to meet my parents for my father's sixtieth birthday, and we spent the week walking around in 40 degree heat, looking at ruins.

On the final evening, after dinner, we drank wine and whisky and Dad asked how the book was going, whether I was making progress, whether the book, as they say, was writing itself. No, I said. Or it is. I don't know. I told him I'd been working on it for so long it was like the book was a part of me. It's like I'm obsessed with this narrative, this pain. I need to let go of it, I said, but I don't know how.

For a while neither of us spoke, but then he leant forward and whispered, Come on, Oliver. Between you and me, was it really *that* bad? Yes, I yelled back, instantly, abruptly. It was *that* fucking bad. Or maybe it was worse. But you weren't there; no one was there, not really, except Maria, and even then—

You only know what I tell you, I said, finally, staring at the ground, breathing, or trying to breathe. You only know these stupid fucking stories that I spend months, years, writing—

We would have been there, Mum said, but we didn't know. Or we knew, but we didn't know it was that bad. I wanted to call, I said, but I couldn't call. I couldn't *fucking* call. I couldn't use a phone. I couldn't do anything. The pain was already so bad, but it could always get worse. I couldn't leave my house, my bed, my room. Not without painkillers. I just felt so helpless, so useless—

We didn't know, Mum said, again, touching my shoulder. It's not your fault, I said, suddenly feeling pathetic. It's nobody's fault—I just want people to *understand*. I want you to *understand*. I want you to know that I'm strong. I'm not the same kid who couldn't pack a dishwasher, who couldn't clean his room, who spilled food all over his face, his clothes. And I might not be a doctor or a paramedic like my sister and brother; I might not have a *real* career, but I'm fucking strong. I'm—a lot of people would have given up; I almost gave up. But I didn't. And I got through it—but even now it's like I still—I can't—writing was the only thing I was ever good at, but I failed. I—

You didn't fail, Dad said. How would you know? You weren't—you weren't there when I was invited to the Brisbane Writers Festival; they flew me up and put me in the Mantra. I had several panels, two readings and a Masterclass to teach, but I couldn't even open my eyes on the plane. All I could do was take painkillers. I couldn't write and I couldn't read, and when I arrived at the hotel the receptionist asked me to fill out some forms and I started trembling trying to hold back the tears. I kept staring at the space between the desk and the ground with the pen in my hand, biting my tongue. All I had to do was write my name, but I couldn't. I couldn't write my name—I couldn't—how do I explain that to you? To anyone? How do I tell you I was a writer at a writers' festival and I couldn't even write my own name?

For a while, no one spoke. Then I said, When I got to my room I thought there had been some mistake: it was so big and surely for one of the more important writers. I wanted to call Maria or I wanted to call you or I wanted to take a photo but I couldn't—I couldn't do anything. I kept telling myself to breathe. I decided to take a shower. Hot water always helped with the pain and I thought if I kept taking hot showers then maybe everything would be okay. So I stood under the water, but then I started thinking about the stories I had to write and the classes I had to teach and the pain that would grow into PAIN, and my legs began to shake and then I wasn't standing, but falling. I fell to the floor, and stayed there. I don't remember for how long. I just put my head between my knees and tried—

Oliver—

Dad—I felt like a fraud, but I knew if I just kept taking painkillers then everything would be okay. I'd take painkillers and go speak about non-fiction or storytelling or being a first-time author, or whatever, but it wasn't me—I was manic, insane. I'd raise my hand, as if in school, and interrupt whoever was talking. I'd turn narratives about why we write into stories about losing my virginity. And I wanted to believe so badly that I was okay that I didn't tell anyone – because for the first time in months, on stage, in front of people, high, I felt normal, like I could do anything. But then the painkillers would wear off, and I would return to my hotel and hide beneath the covers. I'd cry. I'd look at myself in the mirror and wonder what the hell was going on. Eventually, I would sleep, take more painkillers and do it all again.

I remember on that third day, I had to teach the Masterclass, but I didn't know how. I couldn't read any of the writing. So I just brought in a bunch of books I liked, and then told people to open them at random. I told people sentences, those true sentences, the ones that mattered could act like mirrors, and if you held them up at the right angle you could see yourselves in them, and characters from tens or hundreds or thousands of years ago could become your teachers – I told people that if they believed, truly believed in the power of a story then magic and time travel were possible too, and problems became inconsequential because all the problems that ever were had been written about before. And so I watched people search for sentences, and I watched other people copy them out too, and I wanted to grab each one by the neck; I wanted to scream – because they would never know how lucky they were. And I wished more than anything to be like them, then, to be young and curious and beautiful and able – but the thing that hurt the most was realizing that no one gave a fuck, that you were a commodity, that there were terrible books that sold brilliantly and brilliant books that sold terribly, that the whole industry—by the end of the festival I could hardly move; I felt empty, hollow; I just wanted to get on the plane; I wanted to get away from it all; I wanted the pain to go away, but I still had one more reading—I was so nervous; I was shaking; the night before I hadn't slept because I knew I would have to look at the page; I would have to read; I hadn't read for longer than ten seconds for more than three months because each time—and I wished to God that this would be the moment that everything changed, and then I wished for even more things too: I wished to be younger or I wished to be older or I wished to be anyone other than me. I wished my book had never happened—I remember the lady introduced me to the six people waiting for my reading and I put on a brave voice and I smiled and I stared at the page and tried not to cry. I smiled and I read and I told the beginnings of a story, but then the codeine began to join the words together, or my tears made them blurry, or my head snapped or my skull throbbed, or the room shrank, or I was distracted by people leaving—in the taxi, on the way to the airport, I thought, absurdly, how at one point I would have given my life to literature, that I would have died for these letters, but passing the Brekkie Creek Hotel I wondered what the point of it, or anything—

I don't know, I said after a while. People always think the pain is what breaks you. But it isn't. It's the boredom. It's the doctors who don't know and the friends who no longer call. It's realizing that nothing ever changes – that tomorrow will be the same as the days before it and you no longer care if they come.

We paused, then, and I sat with my father; I'd pulled

my hat over my eyes; I was thirty-one years old and I was crying and I didn't want him to see. And then I said, I don't want to make you feel bad – I'm not trying to make anyone feel bad – I just want people to understand. For a long time, with this new book, I wanted to hurt people. I wanted them to feel, for a moment, how I felt, how so many people feel. I wanted to put all my hurt on to those pages and seal them between covers and I wanted to send that out into the world. But I can't write that book. I don't want to write that book. I don't know how. Dad, I had to teach myself to write again, and I'm trying—I'm trying to turn this pain into—I want people to read this book and know that whatever they're going through they can get through it too – because I would have given anything to have a book, a story like—

I felt his hand on my shoulder, and we sat for a long time. You know, he said, when I sat down to read your first book, I was scared. I've never enjoyed those books or movies that make you *feel* things; there's already too much of that shit in this world; it was always simpler to not feel, to be entertained – that's why I always read books with sailing ships on the cover, and sci-fi. To escape. But when I read your book, you made—you made me feel okay. I don't know if I ever told you that. Look at me, he said. You made me feel okay.

And so I looked into his eyes and I saw that he was crying too. Dad, I said – the question already forming, spilling – Dad—I tried to stop, but I couldn't – What happened to us? I asked, no longer daring to look. You and Bear always joke around and laugh and have fun, and you and Brigitte see the world in the same way — all analytical and detailed, but with us, it's like we can never talk, not really. I know you love me, but it's like we're not friends, or it's like we keep missing each other. I've always used jokes to cope with life, with stress, with anxiety, with pain, and you've always used lists or seriousness, and I feel like we don't know how to talk to one another because we're speaking different languages — I admire you so much, and I want to be better friends or even best friends with you. I know I haven't been the perfect son — I took a breath, then, wanting to look up, but being unable to — but I just wondered why we're not—I wondered if you wanted that too.

And so he told me for the second time to look at him. He said, You're my first son. And I love you. I'm proud of the man you've become. But I was a father for the first time too. And looking back, I had no idea what the hell I was doing. No parent does. And maybe I was harder on you than the others, but it was only because I wanted the best for you. I'm the first to admit I could have been there more. When you were young all I did was work. I didn't know how to switch off. I was stressed and trying—

It's okay, Dad, I said. I—

No, he said. Let me finish. When you were four I used to take you to the park and smoke a joint and we'd play soccer together. I don't know why I'm telling you that, but I loved those moments. They were the favourite part of my day. Then he paused and said, I want to thank you for your courage, for this — I know it's not fucking easy. And I want to take some responsibility too. You put me in your writing so much I should have known you were trying to reach out—

We are different people, he said, finally. But we can work on it, together. But I want to have interesting conversations with you, meaningful conversations. I don't give a fuck about Elmsy or Dome Lord or whoever you and Harrison laugh about. Earlier today when we were talking about stories and you told me about endings, about the ways things could end, how conclusions could shine a light over the whole narrative and make you see it new, as if you had and had not been there – that was interesting, and something I'd never thought about before. You've got a lot of pain inside you, he said, pouring more whisky into my glass. I can see that. But you need to use it. Transform it. I'm trying, I said. But I'm scared. Of what? Everything. I went through it all with the first book—I know what to expect, but it doesn't make it any easier. At least while I'm working on it, I have purpose, a plan, but once it's over—once—I don't even know how to write books. The first one was a fluke—the first one—it fucked me up, Dad—it—I don't want that to happen again—it can't happen again—

I pulled my hat down further until Rome disappeared and my father disappeared and I kept it there with my eyes closed until the whole world began to disappear too. I wish I was stronger, I said, finally. I'm a grown man who knows how to do fuck all, except, maybe, one specific thing, but I failed – and I'm so scared of failing that I don't want to try again.

I'm not sure how much time passed after that: a few

seconds? Several minutes? But what I do remember, eventually, is my father clearing his throat, his hand coming across the table, and then a hotness in my chest, a searing openness through my throat, and my hand trembling, moving, slightly, imperceptibly, then all at once, coming to a rest in his.

Even now, it's hard to talk about this moment. Because how do you describe the weight of a son's hand in a father's? How do we talk about being held? When I finally summoned the courage to look up, my father was staring at me, his face almost smiling, or trying to smile, but then not smiling, crying. Here, I said, crying, but now trying to smile too. And then I poured more whisky into our glasses and we drank, holding hands, in silence.

You know, Dad said, after a while. When I was fifteen, I made a promise to myself that I was going to love myself no matter what. I decided I wasn't going to let other people's opinions of me change who I was, and that I would be happy with myself as myself. And maybe that's arrogant or selfish, but I felt like I needed to take a personal stand.

And I realized, at the age of thirty-one, that I'd never done that, that I'd taken myself for granted, that I'd only pretended to have a dialogue with myself, that I had no idea who I was.

***

That night, before I went to sleep, I thought about the last thing Dad said to me, and even now, years later, I can still see us: our eyes teary, arms around one another, and then Dad's voice as he stepped back, his smile, his hands on my shoulders: Write the fucking book, Oliver.

So I did.

The Healer

When you start working for the trains, you hear all kinds of train stories. There were the stories about the guards and drivers who used to go to the pub on their breaks. Whenever management needed someone they would call the pub and tell them to send the least maggot person there. They'd say, We need Barry to run a train out to Richmond, but then the bartender would say, Barry's fuck-eyed, mate. I'll send Jeff. Course this was back in the 70s and 80s and 90s when a job from Central to Waterfall was known as a six-pack: three on the way there and three on the way back. These were the days when being fuck-eyed was just part of the job.

Then there were the stories you read about in the paper. Like the one about the guy who poured a two-litre bottle of Coke over his dick after receiving a blowjob from a stranger on the train. What happened was, they'd met at Port Lakemba train station, and the lady who the man later said had a 'mad body' tapped the guy on the shoulder. I'm horny, she said. Will you fuck me? He declined, but after they boarded she began to masturbate. No one else was on the train, and she masturbated, and she masturbated, and the guy couldn't take it, so he pulled his pants down and approached the lady instead. Then she blew him, and after they were done, he unscrewed the cap on his two-litre bottle of Coke and rinsed himself off. Station staff at the next station found him with his dick in his hands and when police asked him what he was doing he said, I got a blowjob from a stranger on the train and was rinsing my cock off. Later, in Wollongong court, he would say, She was pretty horny and ready to go. Toey as. But then he would say other things too. He would say, I didn't know they had cameras all throughout the train. He would say, How can you go from being so lucky to unlucky in a day? He would say, I don't know.

Then there were the stories you heard in passing. Like the time I walked into the break room and heard Bruce telling everyone how in 1975 he was nine years old and his mum had given him $10 to buy an air rifle from Coles. That's right, he said. Coles. That's how much the world had changed. So he bought an air rifle and when he returned, guess what? His mum gave him another $10 so he could buy one for her too. He told us how they spent their afternoons on the farmlands on the outskirts of Queanbeyan shooting their air rifles at trees, at abandoned cars, at cans. He said at her funeral he dug out the air rifle from beneath the house. And then he shot a single shot. And even now when he closes his eyes he can still see it: he can still see his ma shooting rifles in the dark night air.

My favourite stories were the ones that weren't stories at all. Just the other day this guy with a rat-tail, matching tracksuit and one of those stolen Ofo bikes got on the train, but the train wasn't moving so he just started yelling, Hurry up, cunts! Move it along! Daddy's got somewhere to be!

***

But then there were the stories you'd never tell anyone. One time I asked this driver about the worst thing he'd ever seen. I was fresh, only a few weeks on the job. We'd been laughing and joking about his youth in Mauritius. He'd worked at a luxury hotel and he used to sleep with all the men's wives when the men were at golf. He used to steal all the beers from the kitchen and drink them on the beach in the moonlight with his friends. But now he was staring and I was staring and I knew we weren't joking any more. Then he told me about the sixteen-year-old girl who jumped in front of his train and he told me about her eyes. He told me how they bored into him and then he said, She watched me as she fell, man. And she just stared. And there was nothing. Nothing.

Listen: for a long time I couldn't tell this story, and then when I could I didn't know how.

One evening we pulled into Hornsby station and a police officer asked if she could ride in my cab. Prefer not to ride with the cattle, she said, winking, and then she told me about her day, and how tired she was. I asked if she liked being a cop and she said, Not really. Then I asked what she would be doing if she wasn't a cop, and she said, I don't know. Probably living a life of crime. Seems to work for everyone else. We sat for a while and spoke about Sydney, or old Sydney, before the lockouts, when Oxford Street was packed every night of the week. The lockout laws are just a bullshit scheme to redevelop Kings Cross, I said, and she laughed and said, Yeah. Then she said, Did you ever go to those gay clubs on Oxford Street? I remember going out till 7 a.m. once. Course this was seven years ago. Got out and it was sunlight and I was like, What the fuck am I doing with my life? Sometimes we'd go to the Colombian. Love me a gay boy. There was this guy who wanted to have his first kiss. So my friend, she just went up and pashed him. We used to do mad shit like that all the time. Then her radio made a radio noise and she looked blankly out the window and said, But those days are long gone. Anyway, tell me about your life. Why did you become a guard? It's a long story, I said. We were at Waitara and travelling all stops to Central. Not like I'm going anywhere. So I took a breath and thought about it. I was going to make something up. But I told her this instead.

The day I returned to Brisbane, Mum took me to see the headache doctor. She dropped me outside a tall building and I rode the elevator to the top floor. In the lobby, a receptionist told me to fill out some forms. So I took a pen and I took the paper and I pretended to be normal. I sat in a chair and stared at the page and waited for the pain. I wrote my name and I wrote my birthday and I didn't start to cry. I wrote my address and I didn't try to explain. I began to sweat and I began to shake and the receptionist asked if I was okay.

The headache doctor took me into his office and explained that he wasn't a real doctor but he knew how the head worked. He showed me a model of a head and a model of a neck and then he pushed down on the joints marked C4 and C5 and said words like *muscles* and *knots* and *pressure* and *build-up* and *pain*. He said his practice was experimental and he couldn't promise anything, but he'd had luck treating people with headaches in the past. Besides, he said. You're only seeing me because I'm your last hope, right? You've seen all the doctors. You've had the MRIs. And no one knows what the hell is going on? Tell me I'm right. You're right, I said. You're goddamn right I'm right, he said. My head pounded. Who was this man? I stared into his eyes and prayed he was a healer.

The Healer told me to lie down and the Healer told me to breathe. He said, I'm going to apply pressure to parts of your neck. I need you to tell me if this triggers the pain. Then he pressed down on the back of my neck and it triggered the pain. Then he pushed down on another part of my neck and it triggered the pain. Then he pushed down on another part of my neck and he told me to close my eyes. He applied pressure to the muscle and said that no one, not even doctors, knew how the body really worked. He pushed and he pushed and I felt the man with the shovel return to the spot behind my frontal lobe. He pushed and he pushed and a shovel went WHACK and the pain grew into PAIN and I tried not to cry. The Healer said, I know this hurts, but it's going to be okay, and he pushed and he pushed and I waited and I waited. But then, something extraordinary began to happen. The pain began to go away.

The Healer said, Can you feel that? The bastard's releasing. So the bastard was a muscle and the muscle was releasing. Then the Healer moved to another part of my neck and he pressed another knot and I closed my eyes and saw myself as a little boy. Each night, before bed, I'd say a prayer. I'd say, Please don't let me wake in my own piss tomorrow morning. Amen. But the following morning I'd wake in piss-soaked sheets in my pissy little bed and I'd wonder what I'd done to make God so mad. I'd wonder why he didn't hear me and why he didn't love me and then I'd call myself stupid. I'd punch myself in the bladder and then I'd go to the shower and punch my bladder there too. And then the Healer said, You okay? and I tried to respond but I couldn't respond. How could I? I was still a little boy.

But here's another truth: I just lay on the table and wept. After we were done, the Healer asked how I felt, but I just lay there wiping my eyes. Ten months of pain, and now – I didn't know how to feel. Are you okay? the Healer asked, again. Something had happened, but I didn't trust it. In the past there'd been moments, brief moments, when I thought the pain had gone, but each time it had returned, without warning, with force. So I just lay there, checking for the pain; I kept waiting for it to return. Nothing happened. At some point I took the elevator to the ground floor and walked outside. Brisbane in December. I walked to the middle of the Victoria Bridge and stared at the water. I needed silence, to process, as if by speaking I would jinx it, as if by speaking all the magic would unravel and this new world would become untrue.

But that afternoon my friend Grace called and told me there was a party. She said we were going to take heaps of drugs and get fucked up. She said I could meet all her friends and someone would probably bang me, and then she said that all her friends were hot.

At first, I didn't want to go. That afternoon, I'd walked around in a state of bliss, then paranoia, then confusion. I'd had the migraine for ten months, but now I'd seen the Healer and the migraine was gone. The stillness, the lack of pain, was profound, but the feeling was so new it disturbed me. I didn't trust the pain and I didn't trust the Healer and I didn't trust myself. Even now, years later, I find it hard – I guess I'd had the pain for so long I'd forgotten who I was without it. So I made excuses: I was tired; I had a family dinner. But Grace just cut me off. She said, What the fuck's wrong with you? Stop being such a pussy. I'll see you at seven, and hung up the phone. At first, I laughed. Then, I sat. I thought: maybe there is nothing wrong with me? Maybe the pain *really* is gone?

So that evening Mum and Dad dropped me off at a house in West End. Mum told me she loved me and she told me not to go too hard and she said if I needed anything I could call. I told her I would. I said, Thanks . . . you know . . . for being there. For letting me move back in, and then I made a joke about being twenty-nine and moving back home. But Mum just told me not to be silly. She said, We love having you home. We're here for you. And then she turned around and said, I mean it. We're here for you. I remember burying my face in my hands and wiping my eyes. I'm just so sick of fucking crying, I said. It's bull-shit. Everyone's going to think I'm stoned. But Dad just said, Fuck 'em. Who cares what those arseholes think. Not your problem, and then Mum and I laughed because Dad was calling strangers arseholes again. But then Dad said this, Sometimes, I'm not so good with the whole emotions thing. That's where my wife comes in. But she taught me something long ago. She taught me that you have to be kind and you have to be forgiving and you have to have fun. And I think it's time you had some fun. Then he put a hand on my shoulder and said, And if the pain comes back just leave those arseholes and come have a whisky and play some chess with me at home.

It all came out, then. A mixture of laughter and tears, then more tears. All the fear and relief – I wanted to tell him what it meant, then, those words, but I couldn't. Instead, I just nodded. Cried and nodded. Eventually, I wiped my eyes and got out of the car. Then I walked up the driveway and turned around. They were smiling and waving, and then I was smiling and waving too. It was like I was young again.

I walked down a driveway and into a backyard and Grace introduced me to her friends. They said their names and I said my name and we all drank beer and talked shit in the evening light. Someone sold us coke and someone sold us caps and I thought: shit yeah, because we were gonna get high. We racked up in the living room, and we smoked and danced and laughed, and I smiled because it was like afternoons from long ago. Someone told a story about getting fired from Cold Rock because they fucked their boyfriend and got stoned and trapped in the cold room, and someone else told a story about the dealer who buried and lost 1,000 white heart pills in the side of Mount Coot-tha in 2007, and I listened, and I laughed, and I wasn't in pain, and I didn't think about what I would do if the migraine returned or how I would become a burden to everyone I knew. I didn't think about being useless, and I couldn't remember being afraid, and no one else thought about their pain either. No one else thought about the jobs they hated or the bills they couldn't pay or the people who had hurt them long ago. We forgot about our lives.

And then this happened: Grace pointed at a girl on the other side of the party and asked if I thought she was hot. I giggled and said, Yeah. Then Grace said, Like, you'd bang her, right? If you could? and I giggled again and said, Yeah. Then Grace said, Sweet. Me. You. Her. Sam. Foursome. Later.

HOLY SHIT

She explained that Sam was her boyfriend, and that she'd already spoken to Alex, and that she'd wanted to do this for a while. She said, You're into this, right, and I smiled and nodded. Then Grace said, Fuck yeah. We're having a foursome. Yay!

HOLY SHIT

So Grace walked away and the party went on and I kept imagining the fucking. I told myself that fucking would be happening soon, and I would be part of it. I told myself that the pain was gone and the world was a new world now – a new world full of love, and fucking. I thought how a few days earlier I'd almost jumped in front of a train, but now I was high and invited to the fucking. I laughed at how quick it could all change.

But then more hours passed and I walked to the bath-room and looked in the mirror. I looked cooked, but I wondered if I was cooked enough – for the fucking. I decided I was not. So I returned to the party and asked for coke and asked for caps, but everyone had run out long ago. I asked for Ritalin and I asked for weed, but that was all gone too. So I thought: I guess I'll just get shit-faced starting now. I did a shot of rum and a shot of tequila and I prayed that I wouldn't fuck up. I checked for the pain and the pain wasn't there, and I prayed that it wouldn't return. I prayed that I would be strong. I thought: just be strong, ya bastard, and then I drank some more. I told myself it wasn't a big deal. I was just going to get naked with my new friends. Then I drank a glass of wine and heard my cross-country coach from long ago. I heard him yelling and I heard him hollering and I saw him pointing at me too. He was yelling, you're about as useless as a one-legged man in an ass-kicking contest! But something was different now. It was like he was telling the truth.

And then this happened: Sam and I were in the kitchen drinking and talking like we weren't about to have group sex when Grace started yelling at us from the bedroom upstairs. What was she yelling? This: Get the fuck upstairs you fucking cunts. There's three naked girls in here and we're all going down on each other. Stop being pussy cunts and hurry the fuck up.

HOLY SHIT

And then this happened: Sam yelled back, Coming!!!!!!!!! And then looked me in the eye. He said, Oliver. We've just got to go upstairs and be fucking legends. He poured more rum into our glasses and the rum went inside us. We made our rum faces and walked upstairs.

The room smelled of sex and there were five people in the bed. Everyone was naked and moaning their moans. Sam took off his clothes and dived in the middle, and I sat on the edge trying to take off my shoes. I kept trying to undo my stupid laces, but they wouldn't undo. I thought: Fuck you, shoes, and kicked them towards the wall. I took off my shirt and took off my pants and I thought: well, I guess I'm about to have an orgy now. Then someone kissed my shoulder and someone kissed my neck, and I held my breath because that's where the pain had lived. I held my breath because I hadn't slept with anyone since I'd been with Maria and I kept wondering if she was okay. Hands went on my chest and hands went on my stomach and I thought about our walks long ago. Then I told myself to forget. I kissed someone harder and our bodies pressed together, but I kept checking for the pain. I kept checking my eyes and I kept checking my head and I kept checking my neck, and then I'd check them again because I knew the pain liked to play games. Then hands went on my thighs and hands went on my arse and I told my dick to grow. Nothing happened. I told my dick we were normal now and this was called fun. Then I told my dick to stop fucking around. I told my dick that I wanted to be included and I wanted to be strong, and then I laughed and said, I have to go to the toilet, and left the room.

And now I'll tell you something I've never told anyone: I went to the bathroom and put my hands on the sink and cried. I looked in the mirror. I tried to tell a joke. I knew if I could just relax then everything would be okay. I tried a dick joke but I couldn't think of any, and then I tried a knock, knock joke too. I said, Knock, knock. Who's there? and then I started laughing because I knew it was the saddest joke in the world. Then I played with my dick and nothing happened and I punched myself in the bladder like I used to long ago. I punched myself and felt nothing and then I punched myself again. Someone knocked on the door. I yelled, One second! and flushed the toilet. I smiled and opened the door. This was called playing pretend.

And then this happened: I returned to the room and Grace was standing in the middle of the bed holding a bottle of Chandon. She yelled, Chandon, bitches, and the cork went *pop*, and everyone cheered and got sticky and wet. Someone yelled, Couples or no couples? and someone else yelled, No couples! and this was the part in the orgy when everyone began fucking someone new. I crawled back into bed and pulled someone towards me and we kissed and I prayed that this might be the moment that everything changed. I kissed like I liked it and I moaned like I meant it and then I even grabbed this person's arse too. Nothing happened. Then I kissed harder and pressed together tighter and thought how this was a fantasy I'd had so long ago. Nothing happened. Then I stopped kissing and giggled a little giggle and army-crawled to the other side of the bed.

And if you want to know the definition of loneliness it would be this: leaving an orgy by army-crawling to the other side of the bed. I sat against the wall and put my knees to my chest and listened to all the moans. And I thought about the ten months of moans that I'd moaned too. I thought how I'd moaned for the pain to stop and for the migraine to go away, and then I thought how nothing ever *really* goes away. Then I told myself to shut the fuck up. I put my head between my knees – but I guess it must have looked weird during an orgy because Grace crawled over and asked what was wrong. She put her arm around me and whispered, Hey, what's wrong? You're shaking. And I wanted to tell her but I couldn't tell her. We were in an orgy, and my breathing was going too quickly, and my brain was unable to form words. I wanted to tell her that I felt broken, severed, that I no longer knew who I was, that only a few weeks earlier I'd nearly jumped in front of a train. I wanted to tell her I was different now, that I wasn't the Oliver she'd known in Sydney years before, that I couldn't be. But more than anything I wanted her to know that I longed, begged, to feel whole. I wanted to tell her that I'd had the pain for 300 days – I wanted to excuse, to explain – I wanted her to know if you have pain for long enough it begins to change you. But I couldn't. How could I? How can you tell anyone about the past and sadness and life and expect them to understand truly and completely? So I just sat there and shrugged and smiled and waited for

Grace to leave and for the fucking to end. But Grace didn't leave. It was like she knew. She told me to breathe and she told me that everything would be okay. She told me to lie down and then she lay down on top of me and whispered that this was what puppies did when they felt anxious. They lay on top of one another and that's how they felt safe. So we lay there and she hugged me and I buried my head in her chest. At some point, we began to kiss. We kissed and around us people fucked, and then, eventually, we started fucking too. We fucked our quiet fucks, and we held each other close, and it was like the pain had never happened and there was no one else in the room.

Listen: sometimes when I tell this story people say, Shit. They say, That sounds like a fucking nightmare. They say they could never tell a story like that, but the way I described it . . . it was almost like they were there. Then they laugh and shake their heads and say, Are you all right? It's just *so* sad. But then I tell people to wait. I tell people they have the wrong idea. I tell them that this isn't a sad story, it's a love story. I tell them this story isn't even about me. It's about Grace and Sam and egos dissolving and people loving and trusting with everything they have. I tell them how after the orgy we all sat naked on the deck. The sun was coming up and we drank beer and put ice on our balls and Grace said, Who's the better kisser? Me or Sam? So I kissed Sam, and I kissed Grace, and then I called them both gross. I said they were the same.

Then Sam took me aside and said, I just met you. And you just fucked my girlfriend. And I know we're going to be best friends now. He said, Grace wanted to do this, and I love that woman, and one day I'm going to marry her. He said, I'd do anything for that woman, and one day we're going to have lots of babies. But for now I just do whatever makes her happy because it makes me happy too. We hugged, then, and I knew he was trying to tell me something: that none of this was about him. And I knew that if I wanted to heal then I would have to change too. So I quit writing, and I quit stories. I joined the railway. I became a guard.

Ghosts

But we can never quit stories, not really, not while we're alive. We can only see them for what they are: flashes of light and pain and laughter that travel at breakneck speed from our bodies to our heads that colour all the fucked-up and beautiful things that have ever happened. Ultimately, stories are not for truth: they are for magic and alchemy and waking in the middle of the night and second-guessing; they are for editing and rearranging and talking back. They are bridges to the places that no longer or never existed, and the only reason I'm still writing is because I believe, however childlike, that there might be something on the other side.

Here's a quick story from the other side:

When my cousin, Jackson, was seventeen years old he hung himself. No one knows why. There were no warnings, no signs. One afternoon he was alive, and that evening he was not.

At the funeral, my uncle Tim, Jackson's father, stood in front of 300 people and told stories. He looked at friends and parents and family and he told them the things they already knew but did not know. He told them Jackson had taught himself to tie his shoes and his technique was unlike anything Tim had ever seen. He told them when Jackson was three he made $24 going door-to-door selling macadamia nuts he had collected from his backyard. He told them when Jackson was six he was on a soccer team but he wasn't much of a soccer player so they put him in goal but when the ball came Jackson had gone to piss on a tree. He told them Jackson was cut out for so much more than stopping round balls from entering nets.

And then a video of Jackson played and Tim told us other things too. He told us how he and Jackson's mum, Karen, had life bans on PayPal and eBay because when Jackson was under-age he had used their accounts to import waterproof iPhone cases to sell locally, making thousands. He told us how Jackson had a laboratory in his bedroom where he was constantly creating. He had power tools and test tubes and workbenches he had made himself. Tim told us how they would search for free microwaves on Gumtree so Jackson could disassemble them, and about the evening they drove to a Burger King car park because Jackson had bought potassium nitrate from some guy on the internet. He was sending rockets into the air and building bunkers in his backyard. He wanted to be a rocket scientist, or if that failed an engineer, or if that failed he would just work at

Bunnings. He had plans. Big plans. He was figuring out the world and how things went together; he was destroying the rules and creating something new.

When Tim finished his speech, Jackson's casket was placed on the shoulders of many. People had written messages on the casket. People had written: To the moon, Jackson. People had written: I wish we could have talked. People had written: See you there. Then the casket left the church and 'The Final Countdown' played over the church's speakers. People looked around. People smiled. It was Jackson's favourite song. It played for 4 minutes 55 seconds and we smiled our crying smiles because we realized he would never listen to it again.

After the funeral we sat and recalled our own stories about Jackson: about the rockets he had built out of Lego that were never pictured on the front of the box, and the way he rhymed people's names so that Jo became Jo Po and Dave became Dave Wave, and about the time he ran down his driveway with both hands in the air, smiling. We had just arrived at Gosford from Canberra and we were yelling through our windows, Hi Jackson! but Jackson couldn't hear us because he had already climbed the tree above our heads. He was four years old and swinging by one arm from a tree branch and the wind was going *wooshhhhh* and he was laughing and the world was not full of monsters and there was no pain and the wind was catching his laughter and spreading it over the land like a fever.

Years later, my sister and I returned to Gosford and we sat down for lunch with Tim and Jo and spoke about all the things that had happened and changed in our lives. My pain had gone, mostly, and my sister had become a doctor, and Tim told us about all the ways his life had changed too. Some of the stories we knew. Like the one about how shortly after the funeral Tim began having dreams. Jackson would visit Tim in his dreams and instruct him that he needed to repaint the door, that he needed to build a garden, that he needed a place to sit, to think – there needed to be a bench. But these were no ordinary dreams, for Jackson would tell him the specific types of paint and plants and wood, and when he woke he would find messages scrawled to himself in the night: paint colours and plant names and wood types that he had never heard of, and at Bunnings he would show his scribbled notes, and more often than not the sales attendants would nod and return, smiling – lucky, they would say. We only had one left. And so Tim repainted his door and built his garden and installed his bench, and he told us how Jackson was all around him now, how he felt closer to Jackson than ever before.

And so lunch finished and we drank tea and ate lamingtons and spoke about all the other unexplainable events that had happened in our lives. I told Tim about the ghosts Mum had seen in our house – about the young kids that ran up and down the stairs and the old lady that sat on the brown sofa in my parents' room, and then I laughed because it sounded so *strange*, all this talk of the afterlife, but the way Mum had described it – Oh, they weren't scary! They were innocent, playing! – made it seem beautiful.

Then my sister told the other one about our mother, back when she was studying nursing, and how they had been at the hospital revising for their practical exam. She and a classmate had been roleplaying, taking turns being sick, when the classmate stopped speaking, fixated on something behind Mum's head. For a while, she didn't move. But then she said, I don't mean to alarm you, but sometimes I see things. And there's a man behind you. So Mum looked over her shoulder. She didn't see anyone, tried to play it off as a joke. Come on, she said, smiling, but then, after a while, she asked, What kind of man? He's a tall, old man with a comb-over. He's looking at you lovingly, and smiling. The colour drained from Mum's face. Sound like anyone you know? Yeah, Mum said. That's my dad.

Tim scratched his head, then, and leant forward. He said something similar had happened when he and Mack, his other son, were in Canada several months earlier. They had been in a bar, drinking and talking, when a lady walked up to them. She was holding a Jack & Coke and apologizing for the intrusion, but sometimes, she told them, she received these messages. She said she hoped this wouldn't make them feel uncomfortable, she had no idea if they knew who Jack was, but someone named Jack had told her to buy a Jack & Coke, and to deliver it to their table, and to say that he was watching over them, that he loved them very much, that they shouldn't blame themselves for what happened, and that he was in a better place now. Then she placed the Jack & Coke on the table, apologized once more, wished them a good night and left.

I don't know how long we stared at that drink, Tim said, but eventually I asked Mack if Jackson ever visited him in his dreams. Yeah, Dad, Mack said. All the time. Well, what does he say? Just like, have a heaps good time and that, Mack said. Yeah . . . just like . . . have a heaps good time. At this, Tim looked up and smiled. You know, he said. I thought Mack might have said something more profound than that. But then I realized, maybe, it was the most profound thing of all.

Hope

Let me be clear: this is not a happy story, it will not bring catharsis, but occasionally, on the trains, I heard or witnessed certain events that almost, for a time, made me believe in the impossible, or the unlikely, or in hope, again.

***

Like the time our transport minister was on the TV announcing his plans to turn train stations into shopping malls. He said that once you stepped off the train you could start shopping straight away. Then he made a reference to Shinjuku and another reference to shopping straight away being better than not shopping straight away. Fuck off, you dog cunt, this train guard said, sitting next to me. Then he took a bite of his sandwich, wiped his mouth, looked around and said, again, Fucking dog cunt. Morale seemed high, and as I left he gave me a nod, and I returned it, smiling, ready for another beautiful day.

Or the time at Telopea this guy with a shaved head and a mullet yelled, Check this the fuck out you fucking mad rooter, and he winked at me, then punched a Telstra telephone box.

***

One morning around 4 a.m. we passed Parramatta women's prison and the driver told me I reminded him of his son. You're all ribs and prick, mate. It was raining and we were listening to classical music, taking the train empty out of the city. How old is your son? I asked. He smiled, and told me the bastard was eight.

When I was eight we lived in Canberra, and I fell in love with the girl who lived at the bottom of our street. Her name was Melanie, and the other kids would tease us and sing OLIVER AND MELANIE SITTING IN A TREE . . . K I S S I N G. In truth, I did not mind the teasing, and though my face would turn red, it was not due to embarrassment or shame, but rather, because I wished it was true.

This all happened around the time I met Dean. He was twelve and I was eight and we used to hang out in the park after school. I don't remember what we spoke about – probably skating or girls, all we did then was talk about skating or girls – but one day Dean showed up with a bruise on his face. He was always getting into fights, or talking about getting into fights, so it wasn't that unusual, but I remember that afternoon because instead of talking about the fight he said, Wanna know where babies come from? Where? I asked. Arseholes, he said. We all come from arseholes. He said when two people loved each other they rolled around and grunted and screamed and after they smoked cigarettes. Sometimes, a baby grew in a lady's stomach until it travelled down to where the shit was made, and when the baby had its baby arms and baby legs and baby head and baby feet and baby face it came out the shitter. That's why we're all arseholes, he said. Your parents or teachers will tell you that storks deliver babies, and the Bible will tell you they come out of thin air, but that's bullshit. They're fucking lying. And you know why? Because *they're* arseholes! Then he lit a cigarette and exhaled a bunch of smoke rings into the air, and it was like he wasn't twelve, but forty-five, and I smiled because I knew Dean was the one who could teach me about the world.

A few days later Dean and I were skating around Erindale shops when he asked if I had a girlfriend. I just smiled and shook my head, but then I told him about Melanie. I told him how cool she was and how funny she was and that our school was celebrating Halloween soon. I told him the school was putting on a school dance and a HOUSE OF HORRORS and that I was gonna ask Melanie to go with me. Then I just started giggling and told him I was going to get her flowers. I was going to give her flowers and ask her to the dance. I know it's stupid, I said. But it's what they do in the movies, and then I shrugged and said I wanted her to feel special. But Dean just laughed. He laughed and he laughed and he said that was the stupidest thing he'd ever heard. He said only pussies got girls flowers, and then he asked if I was a pussy. No, I said, but then my face went all red and I stared at the ground because I didn't want him to see. Jesus Christ, he said. Flowers? and then he just shook his head and smirked and put on a high voice and said, I just want her to feel special, before laughing again.

But I did want her to feel special, I thought, walking home, confused, and then I wondered why people were always mean to the ones they liked. I was eight years old, and I wondered why we were still playing pretend.

At some point, though, I summoned or almost summoned the courage to ask Melanie to the school dance. I knew nothing about girls, though suspected Dean knew even less, so I decided to copy those BMX riders at the skate park who always had girlfriends and who, after it rained, rode their bikes quickly around the snake pit, before skidding to a stop in front of their girlfriends along the concrete.

It looked like this: one afternoon, when Melanie and I were riding our bikes home from school, I rode ahead and slammed on my brakes, skidding two, three, four seconds in the dirt. Around the fifth second, ludicrously, I even turned around to see if she was watching, and at that precise moment I came face to face with a magpie. Suddenly, it was squawking, and by the seventh, eighth, and almost certainly by the ninth second, I was no longer turned around because I had fallen face first in the dirt. Are you okay? Melanie asked, arriving next to me, and when I answered that I was she smirked and told me that's what I got for showing off.

My plan had been to impress her with my ability to stop a bike, and then to ask her to the school dance. As a back-up, I had handwritten a note asking more or less the same thing, and while I had abandoned that plan hours earlier, the note, now, lay on the dirt in front of us, the name MELANIE practically yelling at us from the paper. What's that? Melanie asked, and before I had time to answer, she opened it and saw this:

do you want to come to the school dance with me?
yes
no
(circle one)

It seems almost comical, now, to think that I even held out a pencil, that I turned around under the pretence that she required privacy, or time to think, but in reality I was so mortified at having been attacked, at having fallen, at having unwittingly shared my feelings that I simply wished to disappear. At that moment, though, I felt a circle being drawn on my back, and when I turned around and looked at the paper Melanie had circled *yes*.

And so Halloween arrived and we went to the HOUSE OF HORRORS. The teachers decorated the gymnasium with bloodied sheets and dangling skeletons, and Melanie and I followed a path beneath the stage and people jumped out from the places we couldn't see and scared us wearing masks. We held hands in the dark and clung to one another; we screamed, but when we emerged from that horrible place our hands were still touching and it felt like they were talking to one another. We were in year four, and this was called: love.

Listen: during those ten months I had the migraine, I spent a lot of time lying in bed thinking about all the stories I wanted to tell but could not tell, and did not know why. I would lie there in a sort of catatonic panic with my eyes closed, trying to remember what I had started calling *the before*. I would think about Canberra and Melanie when we were young, about her brown hair that whipped in that dry wind as we rode our bikes to school, and about Dean and that Nike swoosh he'd shaved into his head beneath his undercut so his dad wouldn't know. Occasionally, when the pain was too strong, or if I hadn't left the house in some time, or if I'd taken too many painkillers, or if I just couldn't picture them, see their faces, I would simply invent, and this inventing became a sort of game, a way to travel, to exist, to cope. And perhaps, I think now, this is why certain stories exist, because they allow lifelines to the past, to when we were kids and our imaginations kept us alive.

One afternoon Melanie and I rode our bikes to the library. I'd told her that Dean had said babies came out the shitter, and she'd told me that was the stupidest thing she'd ever heard. She said they came out the vagina. She said we should go to the library. She wanted to prove that it was true. So we rode our bikes down the side of the highway; I had a black Apollo BMX, and Melanie had some mountain bike with cobwebs in the spokes, and as we passed the BMX track I started thinking about Dean, and the time he punched that guy in the face.

We'd been at the BMX track all afternoon, and Dean kept telling me about his new girlfriend, Stephanie. He kept telling me how hot she was and how they stayed up sometimes drinking his dad's rum. We just put water in it, and the old cunt never knows, he said, and then he asked if I knew what a blowjob was. I told him I did. Yeah? he said. What is it then? It's when, you know . . .

and then I went all red and said, It's when two people blow air towards each other, and Dean laughed so hard he nearly fell off his bike. Then he rode down the hill to lap the track again.

For a while, I just sat there calling myself names. Stupid. Idiot. Then I punched myself in the stomach and said, Fucking shitty. But then something else happened. These two guys arrived, and one of them said, Is this your bag? I nodded. Then he opened my bag and said, This your wallet? And I nodded again. Then he took the wallet, said Cheers, and walked away. I tried to move, to call for help, but I couldn't.

Eventually, Dean came back and asked what was wrong. He asked why I was crying, and then he laughed and said, Jesus, I'll tell you what a blowjob is, just relax. But then I started pointing at the two guys walking off into the distance. I told him how they'd robbed me, and how I'd let them, and then I punched my stomach and said, I'm such a fucking idiot, and punched myself again. But then Dean said, Hey. Hey! Take it easy. He put his arm around me and said, Give me a second. Then he got up and I watched him ride towards them. I watched him crash-tackle the bigger guy to the ground. Punch. Then the other guy was on the ground. Punch. Punch.

The fuck's this? Dean asked when he got back. He'd opened my wallet and had removed the only thing in it: a library card. You were crying because someone stole your library card? For a moment I wasn't sure why I was crying, though probably it had something to do with shame; I'd let someone rob me, but then Dean laughed and said, You fucking loser, and I even began smiling, then laughing too, because it seemed funny, suddenly, that we should care so much about libraries, literature, books; it seemed absurd, there, in the mid 90s, in Canberra, that anyone would knock anyone out just so someone could read.

At the library we walked to the adult section, and I kept seeing signs that said FICTION and NON-FICTION and POETRY and HISTORY, but I couldn't see any that said SHIT or ARSEHOLES or BABIES or BIRTH. I think I said something stupid like, Well, I guess you're right because there's no arsehole section, but Melanie just smiled and said, Really? Seems like you're standing in it. We were eight, sure, but we weren't idiots. No kids are. We knew how the world worked; we knew you had to joke. I remember, after, she took my hand and we walked to a deep corner of the library. Then she bent down and selected a book. The book was called *Where Do Babies Come From,* and we sat together reading it on that library floor. I'm sure I read it, or tried to read it, though I don't remember what it said, could only stare at the pictures, my palms sweaty, lips upturned, unable to stop smiling. We were young, but we liked each other, and it felt special to be sharing that book, and we knew it. At some point, Melanie pointed to a diagram and said, See, the vagina. Then we laughed and she called

Dean an idiot again. I couldn't wait to show Dean. I couldn't wait to tell him that he was wrong.

The next day, in class, I couldn't sit still. I kept thinking about Dean and what I would tell him. In some ways, I knew it was a test; he was thirteen, and he was always calling me a pussy or a baby or a dickhead or an idiot, but now he would see me as an equal; now he would see me as a mate.

But when I arrived at the skate park, Dean was sitting with Stephanie; I hadn't planned on Stephanie being there, and I didn't know what to say. I didn't know whether I should come right out with it, or just play it cool. So I did a head nod, or I said, What's up, or maybe we slapped hands. At some point, though, I sat; no one spoke, maybe thirty seconds passed, and then Dean said, So, like, what do you want? I remember laughing, I knew what I wanted to tell him, but still, it seemed too rushed. Besides, how do you tell someone out of the blue that babies come out of vaginas and not the shitter? So I panicked; I started rambling; I started telling them what I'd learned at school. I told them how in science class our teacher had told us about Darwinism and how some spiders ate other spiders for food. Then I told them how we were literally made of stars. I told them that when the universe started there was only hydrogen and a little helium and barely anything else, and that stars took the hydrogen and turned it into helium and the helium into carbon and oxygen and iron and sulphur. And then I said, Guess what we're made of? and I did a wink face and told them carbon and oxygen and iron and sulphur. I told them that when stars died, they got super fat or they joined with other stars, and when they got heavy enough they exploded and that was called a supernova. Then I shrugged and said it was cool because it had the word *super* in it. Then I looked up because I wanted him to know we were the same, that we were as old as each other, that we were as old as the whole universe.

But when I looked up I realized he wasn't listening. They were making out, and then Dean grabbed Stephanie around the cheeks wineglass-style and called her *Steph-fanny-feeler* like he always did, and she just laughed like she always did too. She just laughed and sat a bit closer and then Dean told one of his stories where his dad told him to do something and he told his dad to shut the fuck up. Then Dean turned to me and said, Sorry, what? and I said, What? and he said, Shut the fuck up. Then Stephanie laughed even louder. They were laughing so hard it was like they were a single person laughing at the whole dumb world.

And even now, twenty-two years later, that's all I've ever wanted: someone to laugh with at the whole dumb world.

So that evening I asked Mum why people behaved the way they did. I asked her why people were mean and why people were cruel and why they laughed and made others feel bad. I told her that when Dean and I were together we always had heaps of fun, but whenever we were around others he made me feel shitty. Then I asked her why anyone would do that: why would anyone make anyone feel like they didn't exist? Mum told me she didn't know. I told her the world was so stupid sometimes. It was like there were all these rules you had to follow that didn't make sense. Then I started breathing all heavy and asked her why I still pissed in my sleep. I told her I was eight years old, and I was too old to be pissing in my sleep. I told her that each night before bed I'd say a prayer. I'd say, Please don't let me wake in my own piss in the morning, amen. But each morning I'd wake in my piss-soaked sheet in my pissy little bed and I'd wonder what I'd done to make God so mad. I'd wonder why he didn't hear me, and why he didn't love me, and then I'd call myself stupid. I told her I just wanted to wake how Dean woke, how everyone woke. I just wanted to be normal. Then I told her how Dean had started inviting me to spend the night at his house. He had these sleepovers where you stayed up and played *Doom* on the PC or watched *Rambo* on his big TV. I told her I wanted to go so bad, but I couldn't go. I couldn't go because—and then I started crying because my stupid shitty body—I told Mum each time he asked I kept making excuses. It was family night; I had homework; we were having chicken. But over the past weeks I had come up with even more excuses too. I told him an uncle had died and there was a funeral. I told him it was Dad's birthday. But now I was running out of birthdays and I was running out of funerals, and then I punched my bladder like I did when no one was around. I breathed and I breathed and I punched myself again, but Mum caught my arm and held it against her leg. We sat for a while, then, my stupid tears going into her dress. I tried to free myself, but not really. And then I just stayed there being held. You know, she said, after a while, you're going to meet a lot of dickheads in your life, and they're going to try and make you feel bad, but it's only because, usually, they're hurting too. But the first thing you don't want to do is beat yourself up. Then she asked if I could keep a secret. She told me most people didn't learn this secret until they were much older, and some people never learned it at all, but her dad had taught her this secret, and now she was going to tell me too. Then she said, The only person who gets to control how you feel is *you*. Most people spend their entire lives hurting, or being hurt, but that hurting only brings more hurt until your whole world becomes pain. But more than anything, she said, don't take it all so seriously, and don't forget to be kind. So no more hitting, okay? I nodded, and told her I would try. You know, she said, after a while, I think you're brave for talking about your problems, and then, finally, I smiled because my mum thought I was brave, and I knew if someone else believed it then maybe it was true.

And now I want to tell you something.

You're brave. You're all so brave.

That night, as I went to sleep, I put on a brave face and pretended I was older. I pretended I could control all the things inside me and I could control how I felt. I knew the world had no time for pussies, and I pretended I could change. And then I felt something happening. I turned on the light and looked at my legs and I saw that they were growing, and my chest was growing, and my arms were growing. I looked at my hands and they were man's hands now. They were sweaty and dirty and they were holding AK47s. And I saw my clothes were different too. I was wearing a black singlet. There was a bandana around my head. Then a voice from on high said, Whatever possessed God in heaven to make a man like Rambo? and I laughed because I was Rambo now. I knew being brave just meant playing pretend.

**

Here's the truth: none of this happened, or some of it did, but not like that. Throughout those ten months, I spent most evenings lying awake, and to keep myself sane I would return to those places that existed in *the before*; I would relive a life that happened, and did not happen, and explore those worlds from the confines of my bed. Partly, it was out of necessity – the pain was immense, crushing, but in that other place, if I tried hard enough, I found it possible to escape. Mostly, though, it was out of desperation. Humans, migraines and stories share the commonality of sequence: they have beginnings and middles. They have ends. For ten months my story had no end, and my inability to write, to use screens, to read was an attack on my own imagination from a part of myself that, I suppose, tried to protect itself by destroying who I was.

In something of a plot twist, I recognize that, in death, part of me, or the deep, primal me, would have celebrated, for there no longer would have existed a reason to be afraid. Towards the end, however, that's what scared me the most: because each time, emerging from those narratives, it became harder to return to that increasingly surreal place known as the real world. One day, when that return from *the before* became unbearable, and I was unable to picture what I called *the after*, I simply stopped. By then, I had been unable to write or read stories for nearly nine months, but this meant I forgot how to tell stories entirely, and so I lived within the limitations of the migraine, which meant I forgot how to escape.

Here's a quick story from *the before*: Melanie had dark hair and dark eyes and didn't take any shit. I knew she didn't take any shit because one time Dean called Stephanie *Steph-fanny-feeler* and Melanie told Dean to shut the fuck up. That was the kind of girl Melanie was: she was the kind of girl who told the fuckheads to shut the fuck up.

But she was more than that too. One day, she started wearing lipstick to school. I guess word got out that we liked each other, because in homeroom people began elbowing me, and saying she had worn lipstick for me. They began singing OLIVER AND MELANIE SIT-TING IN A TREE K I S S I N G. I remember blushing and looking at the floor, but then, in front of everyone, Melanie said, So what? Maybe I do like Oliver, and she planted a kiss on my cheek. That night I told Mum about the kiss and how I'd walked around in a daze. It was in front of everyone, I said. I told her I'd never seen any-one act like that. Like what? I don't know, I said. I guess, brave.

By then we were spending most of our morning teas together. We would sit on those old tractor tyres and trade the snacks that our mums had packed us: Dunk-A-Roos for Apricot Delights, Roll-ups for Space Food Sticks. Some of the boys and I would throw the flying fox from one end to the other, trying to break it, and one day I even did, snapping the metal clean off.

That day, at lunch, I decided I was going to ask Mel-anie to the school dance. I walked to the bubblers where she sometimes hung out with Claire, but she wasn't there. Then I walked to the flying fox where we spent morning teas together, but she wasn't there either. Even-tually, I walked to the end of the oval where the grass sloped down towards the fence. This was where Court-ney and Rachel and Laura hung out, where they smoked cigarettes, down where the teachers couldn't see, next to the road. They'd know where Melanie was. They were her friends.

But just before I came into view I heard the girls talk-ing so I hid behind a tree.

Did you see Melanie?

All that make-up.

I heard her dad picked her up.

She looked like a whore.

Like a clown.

Like a freak.

I remember the world stopped, then. No sounds, no laughter, nothing decided: just that dry Canberra heat on that dead Canberra grass and the surprised, frozen, almost happy look on each of the girls' faces, and a boy about to decide what was inside him, whether he would act, whether he was brave. It seems stupid, now, to tell you about my heart, how scared I was, how it was beating. Two hands, and my body pressed against that tree trunk. I had an idea of myself, that when it came down to it I would be courageous, the way Melanie had shown herself to be. Perhaps I was scared of the girls – they were cool and mean and their judgement terrified me – or maybe, abruptly, I saw how ugly the world was, these friends who were meant to be friends talking all shitty behind each other's back. But in reality I knew it was something else. My inaction terrified me and, in that moment, I realized I was weak, that I had no idea who I was. At some point, the world resumed. The girls began to laugh, and I watched them, hiding. They laughed and they laughed, covering their mouths the way people do when they want everyone to see. And then the bell rang, and they ran off, and we all went to class.

In Brisbane, in the days after I saw the Healer, I sat at my desk for the first time in ten months and tried to write about the first girl I ever loved. I tried to write about the bike rides we took, and how she kissed me on the cheek once, and how one day her dad picked her up from school. It was a sad story, one that I'd never told, but I had so much anger inside me that I wanted to hurt, to grieve. In my head, I saw the pictures, the scenes, but each time I tried my body tensed up and my breath stopped breathing and I found it hard to open my eyes. I was no longer in pain, or constant pain, but each time I sat at the computer those electrocutions and stabs returned. So I made fists. I squeezed. I told myself that the pain was gone and that I could look at a computer and that I was better now. I told myself that it was okay to return to *the before* and that I could write and tell stories again. I thought about Melanie and all that happened and I tried to be like her. I tried to be brave. But I couldn't: the screen and the story represented a portal to those spaces where the pain lived, and I didn't want to go back. We're going to look for two minutes, Mum would say, and then, together, we would open our eyes and stare at the computer. Eventually, we worked our way from five to ten, then twenty minutes, but, horrifically, indiscriminately, the pain would reappear and I would return to bed, burying my face beneath a pillow, holding it there and pushing it down, then more until I couldn't breathe.

Pain without end can be demoralizing, but stories without conclusion can be savage too. That afternoon I went to Melanie's house, and on the way there I stopped at a petrol station and bought her flowers. I wanted to make sure she was okay, and maybe, if it felt right, ask her to the school dance, but, more likely, I wanted to absolve myself of some personal guilt too. I wasn't sure if I was going to tell her everything; clearly, something had happened, but I didn't want to make her more upset by telling her all the stupid things her friends had said. At the same time, it felt important to convey that I'd acted like a coward. So I stood on her porch and rang the doorbell. I held the flowers in front of me, the petals shaking, slightly, in my hand. At some point, her dad answered the door, but he didn't look like he normally did: his eyes were downcast and his voice was full of gravel. He thanked me for the flowers, turned his back, and then began weeping too. I tried to say something; I'd never seen a grown man cry before, and I didn't know what to do, so I just did what my parents did when my brother or my sister or I were sad: I gave him a hug. He thanked me, and told me to follow him inside. Melanie's upstairs, he said, or tried to say, and then he disappeared to another room. I remember walking up the stairs, slowly – something terrible was about to happen, or had already happened, or was about to be revealed, but each time a stair creaked I couldn't help but smile. I guess, deep down, it all just felt so *real*, like those movies I had seen on the TV. But when I knocked on the door, I stopped smiling because

Melanie was sobbing. Eventually, she opened the door. For a while, she didn't say anything, and we simply sat together on her bedroom floor. She's gone, she whispered, finally. Who? I almost whispered back, but the way she looked at me, I knew exactly who. Oh, I said. And then, the world slowing, Oh.

Melanie's mum died that morning. She had cancer, and I guess Melanie didn't want anyone to know. Not long after, she and her dad left town and I never saw them again. I suppose they wanted a fresh start; the house, maybe, the memories were too much. Sometimes, you just have to get out.

The afternoon before she left, she invited me to her house and we watched Baz Luhrmann's *Strictly Ballroom* on that same bedroom floor. The end was coming, and we didn't want to talk about it, so we just sipped the Cokes she'd grabbed from the fridge. I wanted to tell her how much she meant to me, how much I valued her, loved her, because I did, I loved her, and I felt for her, and I couldn't comprehend that, suddenly, she was going away. I wanted to say something, heroic, memorable. I guess I'd never really told her how I felt. But instead, I told her I liked that she had stopped wearing make-up. You don't need it, I said. You're pretty as it is. Melanie smiled, then, a smile I can still see now. And in the movie, Tara Morice began to sing 'Time After Time', and the characters danced. Then Melanie leant forward and said, You know, I meant what I said that day in the classroom. I do like you. But I wasn't wearing make-up for you. It was for my mum. It's stupid, she said, looking down, but the make-up was hers, and I thought if I wore it I could keep her alive.

***

When are you going to stop writing sad stories? my dad asked me, earlier that day, when we were walking around Rome. I liked your old stories, the ones you wrote when you were just starting out, the one about the boy who dressed in a tiger suit and ran around the city saving lives. We were standing out front of the Colosseum, and I shrugged, shielding the sun from my eyes. I don't know, I said, I guess when I've said all I have to say. But what I wanted to do, what I should have done, was told Dad to read the story again. Come on, I wanted to say. You knew Melanie. You knew her mum. She didn't die. You were *there*.

Cowardice, I wanted to say to my dad, then, now. It was a story about cowardice. Fiction, absolutely. But more or less true. Sure, I'd say, Melanie wore make-up to school, and she kissed my cheek once, but her mum never died of cancer – that happened to another friend's mum in high school. And all that stuff about hiding behind a tree, about listening to Melanie's friends talk shit behind her back, about being weak, selfish: invention too. But the themes, I'd say, smiling, though trying not to, that same smile I'd smiled in the story when everything felt so *real*. The themes. And then, maybe, I would have told him about that day, that sunny afternoon, at the end of 2015, when I walked to Central station and nearly jumped in front of a train. How it was a day like any other: high-school kids laughing, flirting; old men reading newspapers, mothers pushing prams, businessmen staring at phones. Just a step, I told myself. Just one. I didn't want to die; I just wanted the pain to go away.

Cowardice. Though perhaps, if I'd been better at communicating, I would have tried to explain my limited understanding of storytelling: that in fiction, it's not only possible, but mandatory, to invent, that we *create* cause and effect, that when a story is told convincingly, especially those boring, sad ones, we transport the reader to another world where fathers and sons understand what the other is trying to say.

Of course, life, or the so-called real world, is more cruel. Sometimes people fall in love and never see each other again. Other times, relatively unknown, mediocre writers suffer migraines that don't go away, and they imagine killing themselves. Occasionally, they almost try.

Here's the truth: there was a girl named Melanie who lived at the bottom of my street. We were eight years old, and we were in love. One afternoon, while watching *Strictly Ballroom,* she kissed me on the cheek, and then there was a *For Sale* sign in her yard, and I never saw her again. No cause, or a cause I didn't understand, huge effect. I remember the day she left I walked around the house, the street. My heart felt hot, something searing, like there was a hole in it. I walked to the park. I sat on the slide and went down the slide and I sat on the bark. I stared at the trees. Someone had spray-painted Xs on the trees and I knew what they meant. I knew Dad was right and I knew the world was bullshit because these weren't the Xs you find at the end of a love letter. These weren't the Xs that told you there was buried treasure somewhere. These were the Xs that meant everything goes away.

A sad memory, sure, but the fact that I can write it now makes it a happy story too.

Perhaps it's best to end like this: when you tell someone about a migraine, they usually shake their head and laugh. They tell you they know all about them; they used to get one occasionally, or their mum or dad did, and they know how awful they are. Sometimes they mention how they nursed a loved one through an episode or two. They tell you how they watched them suffer, how they couldn't get out of bed, that you can't just take a Panadol for one, they know that, that all you can do is wait: a couple of hours, a day at most. And you nod, thinking about the waiting, and they smile and you return it because, more or less, the pain has been understood. But just once, you want to shake them; you want to smack them in their stupid face. You want to say, the pain was *nothing* like that. Ten months, you want to say. *Ten.* As if stating a fact could make people understand. But it doesn't, and you don't, and instead, you keep smiling, and you try again, with another metaphor, with a story.

Circles

Let's start over: the migraine had gone, mostly, but I didn't trust it. I was twenty-eight, and broke. I'd left Brisbane and returned to Sydney, and had little, if any, practical, employable experience. That I was pain-free, initially, felt like nothing short of a miracle, though, in the end, certain activities – looking at computers or phones or screens or anything up close, sitting in a chair – would trigger a relapse so violent I would forget the pain had gone at all. I had become a reader who no longer read and a writer who no longer wrote: the two things I felt, above all else, I knew vaguely how to do.

But I kept trying. One day, I took two painkillers and opened my computer. I typed Sydney + No experience + Full time into Google. Sydney Trains was hiring train guards. I speed-typed an application, and sent it in. I don't remember what it said. I passed two exams, a role-play, three interviews and, miraculously, a drug and alcohol test. Three months later I began train school. Six months later I became a guard. Eight months later I began to write, again, in pencil, in fragments, between stations, while working on the train. I wrote on the back of old train diagrams, and placed them in the stack on my desk when I got home. On good days, I made jokes. On bad days, when the migraine returned, I cried. I didn't know it, then, but I needed time to think, to process, to go around and around, physically, mentally, without going anywhere at all. My base was Central, and I travelled in circles, over 200 kilometres a day. I no longer cared for books, and I'd given up being a writer, but I knew if I could tell it, trap it, here, for me, just once, then maybe everything would be okay.

That first day, after I relieved the guard from that suicide at Hornsby, I returned to Central and sat in the break room, staring at the show *Think Tank* on the TV. The game wanted to know the name of Richard Flanagan's Man Booker Prize-winning novel. All the words were there except for the end word, and you had to pick the end word. I remember the contestant laughed and said he should know this one; he was a writer, but then he went silent. He scratched his head. Then he apologized and said he didn't know. Books? one of the train guards said. Who gives a flying fuck? and then he walked out of the room.

I remember that first train, first lap around the Quay. I'd been sitting in the break room when another train guard offered me half of her lunch. I protested, told her I had already eaten, but she just snorted. Skinny thing like you? Couldn't hurt to have two lunches. Go on, eat up. And so we sat, talking about the suicide rate on the network, eating her chicken and rice and salad that she had divided in two, when my phone rang. Platform 17, the voice said. A run number was given; he told me to take her around the Quay.

I left the break room and walked to platform 17. Brand-new uniform, bright orange bag, train keys dangling by my side. The sun shining; I waited in the middle of the platform with my train-issued speed dealer sunglasses on, smiling, my stomach in knots. I suppose I felt a mixture of pride and terror – it still seemed absurd that anyone had hired me, that I'd received all my qualifications, that all that massaging and stretching and manipulating had worked, that the migraine had, mostly, remained at bay. In many ways, I think now, I felt how I so often felt as a writer: lucky, but also an imposter, as if at any moment the big boss might march up that platform, or into my room, and take those keys or my laptop away. Had a couple dickheads riding scooters up and down the carriage, the guard said, handing the train to me. But they got off at Redfern, so you're sweet. No worries, I said. Hooroo, he said, and then he was gone.

Peak hour, eight carriages, two thousand people per train. I checked the departure time, then positioned myself halfway out the door. I looked right, left: I saw school kids flirting, laughing, listening to music; old women arm in arm, helping one another on to the train. A day like any other, I thought. Eventually the signal light illuminated. Station staff blew their whistles, flags raised and I pressed the warning announcement that told the world the train would soon close its doors. Nothing happened. So I pressed it again. Still, nothing. I remember a sinking feeling, followed by short, sharp breaths. Panic. Irrational, but real. My legs, suddenly, began to shake. The station staff blew their whistles, and I went over the procedures we had learned in the classroom and with our trainers a million times before. Keys in—keys, I said, to no one. But where—I tapped my belt where they had been hooked only a moment before, but they were not there. Several moments later, absurdly, I tapped again. I'm sure I froze, although perhaps I began to pace; either way I was no longer part of the external world, but rather observing a grotesque simulation of the future, one in which trains upon trains upon trains had backed up causing extensive delays, news reports, persons interviewed. What a complete moron, one said. First day on the job, and he couldn't even find his keys. My bloody chicken went cold, added another, holding up his Coles bag.

At some point, the station attendant said, Looking for these? then pointed at my keys in the door. Fucking hell, I said, red-faced, sweating. Finally, keyed in, I played the door announcement. Then, I closed the doors and gave the driver the bell. As the train began to depart, the station attendant said, New? I nodded. I've seen worse, she said, grinning. First week most of you can't even find the right platform.

It was not a question of competence that made me panic – I had only to put my train keys into the train – but a fear of *appearing* incompetent, of breakdown, of failure. I guess, if you looked at it square, it was a question of ego. As our train moved towards Town Hall, I took a breath and tried to steady my voice. I cleared it, trying to swallow all the jitters, and attempted to make it new. I knew all the rules, the regulations; there was no need to be nervous – I knew what to do. It was almost funny when you thought about it: fucking up on the first day in front of everybody, like one of those dreams where you turn up naked and have to give a speech in front of the whole school. A lot like the migraine, I thought. A lot like my first book.

The train accelerated, and we entered a tunnel. In class, we'd practised announcements using our hands as telephones. We'd been coached in pronunciation, elocution; we'd been told, if we wanted, we could even make it a little funny too. G'day legends, I'd said, practising in front of the class. Next stop is Town Hall, but for all you out-of-towners, hot tip: we call Town Hall . . . The Little Dipper! Put that in your Sydney pipe and smoke it. This is the Train Lord – signing out! It had been a good day;

no pain; a few gags; I'd even been able to look at the iPad for longer than a few minutes; at lunch, I might have even read a book. If Maria was here, I thought, she'd be impressed. No more closing my eyes on the train because I couldn't look out the window; no more deep breaths; no more writing, or trying to be a writer; no more pain, or some pain, but, mostly, not in my head. Attention, customers, I said, announcing where we were and where we were going, then repeating it, a requirement of the job, sure, but also because, from my writer days, I knew if you repeated something then it would come true.

The train pulled into Town Hall: hot air, dust, kids squealing. I went through my checklist: train on the platform, check. No obstructions, fires, no people falling between the gap. Check. My new life: no thinking, or thinking only what we had been taught. I opened the doors. A short man in a suit: I don't give a fuck what Harold said. The deal's going through Monday. Two teenagers holding hands. A grandmother lighting a cigarette at the end of the platform. A good scene for a book, I thought. Nothing special, nothing happening, but that's what I liked about it. A beginning, everything in front. Then a man boarded the train, looked at me, and yelled, You're late.

Stupid, but in that moment, my blood boiled; I wanted to yell something back, something dumb, something antagonistic – I wanted to *explain*, but by then he had already boarded the train, everyone had, and the station attendant and I were the only people left on the platform. So I took a breath, and blew my whistle. Closed my doors. Gave the driver the bell and our train lurched forward.

But I kept thinking about it – you're late. I kept thinking about it at Wynyard when I received a call from head office asking why our train had lost three minutes at Central, and I kept thinking about it at Circular Quay when I closed the doors and a guy ran at the train, hands in the air, crazy person style, and the station attendant whispered, Not today, fuckhead, then gave me the flag to proceed. I kept thinking about it at St James when I stared at my train-issued wristwatch because I'd never worn a wristwatch before. And I kept thinking about it at Museum too. I kept thinking about it because the man was right: I was late, and I wanted to know why. People boarded and people disembarked and I kept thinking about those ten months that I wanted to write but could not write, and about those trains that I wanted to catch but could not catch because of the lights in the carriage and the world that moved too fast beyond the window, and about those nights that I lay awake begging for the migraine to go away. Go away, I'd said. Go away. I kept thinking about those mornings that I took painkillers and tried, but failed, to keep the pain hidden from my friends – I didn't want to be treated differently, and some part of me thought, or hoped, that if I kept pretending to be normal, then, one day it might be true. I kept thinking about it, approaching Central, how absurd it all was, how every now and then someone would thrust a phone in my face and tell me to look at some photo or video and I would excuse myself to the bathroom to take more painkillers, or cry, or how in the supermarkets I had begun to protect myself by walking around the aisles with my eyes closed for five, then ten seconds at a time. I kept thinking how I'd told myself it was the lights, that they had a bad flicker rate, which now seems ludicrous, but even so, I would walk around as if blind, occasionally opening my eyes, smiling, absurdly, at friends when I saw them – for sure I'll see you at the party later – only to return to that private hell once they'd left.

I kept thinking about it when I was relieved at Central, how mostly, no matter what I did, the pain was simply indifferent, that it was all I could do to stand up.

I kept thinking about it when I quit the trains two years later: like electrocution, I'd told people. But worse. A shovel. Burning. Dulling.

And I'm still thinking about it *now*. I'm still thinking about it because I have so many questions. What happened? Why was I late? Why? And the only reason I am still writing this book is because I think, or hope, however absurdly, that one day I might find the answers inside.

Miracles

Sometimes, the trains felt almost spiritual. One day, in a taxi on the way to relieve another suicide, a driver told me he'd never had a fatality. Fifteen years, he said, not one. But then he told me about the time he traded his shift to another driver, and that driver had someone jump in front of his train. The guilt, he said, looking at his hands, shaking his head – you can't describe it. It was a sunny day, not much traffic; the radio played Shania Twain; I remember we passed a petrol station that said unleaded petrol was 139.99. You don't have to look at it, he said, finally. When we get there, I mean. Sometimes it's better just to look away.

When we arrived the police had cleared everyone out, and I stared at that blue and white tape, trying to not look beyond. The girl dropped her wallet and tried to retrieve it, the cop said, shielding his eyes from the sun. She jumped down on the tracks, but then she couldn't get back up. Then the train came. So she lay flat against the staunching, and prayed – or that's what she told me anyway, he said, grinning, after we arrived and moved the train on. No fatality? the driver asked. No fatality, the cop said, his gold tooth glinting. Well shit, the driver said. How about that.

Luck, a train guard said in the break room, a few days later. No two ways about it. And stupid. The needle could have hooked his leg, his arm – he could have lunged. Besides, can you even, you know, *legally*, drop-kick someone in the chest?

There had been another incident: at the end of a shift, one of the guards had found a person drunk, sleeping on the seat. The guard was tired – he'd worked nine hours, and still had another hour to commute home. Generally, we'd been instructed not to touch the clientele, especially in what management called altered states of consciousness. Beyond the legal ramifications, most people weren't happy when a stranger woke them at 1 a.m. on a Tuesday night on a train seat. So the guard said, Wake up. He clapped his hands. He blew his whistle. Eventually, he shook his shoulder. Wakey, wakey. At this, the guy woke. The way I heard it, at first, he looked almost serene. No hate, no sadness. Not rested, sure, but the eyes, he said, almost pure – angelic even. But then, he grew confused. There was some mumbling, a gargling sound. And then, he was on his feet. Fists up, knees bent. Fighter stance. And in his hand was a needle. So what did the guard do? He lured the man into the main vestibule, grabbed the handholds above him, and drop-kicked the guy out the door.

He's a bloody hero, another guard said. The guy's got a needle. You ever tried talking to a needle? So he did what he had to – he drop-kicked the cunt in the chest.

You should have seen the CCTV footage, another

said. The way he flew. It was almost *magical* – the train, the empty platform, and then the body, flying.

It wasn't a few days later that a guard in the break room turned to me and said, So I bought a fucking microwave. They wanted $296. I said no way. I said $246. I said I get it online for $246. So I got the fucking thing for $246. 1100 watts. Got a fucking timer. High speed. High power. Got those fucking – then he started clicking his fingers trying to remember – fucking knobs. Really makes a difference. Less dead time during the heating period. Been lusting after it for months. Then he showed me a picture of the microwave, sat back in his chair and put his hands behind his head.

I liked him, these interruptions – so much of the job was spent alone: in guard compartments, on platforms, in train yards, and while I rarely initiated conversation, in many ways I yearned for it: the humour, the connection. Wait, I said, leaning forward. Did you say $246 . . . for high power . . . and the knobs? You heard me, he said, grinning. Papa's got a magic tongue, and he uses it to make miracles.

Sometimes Maria and I would stay up late and talk about the miracles we had seen in our own lives. One night I told her that my grandfather had survived the

Holocaust. He was studying at the University of Amsterdam, and he refused to sign allegiance to the Nazi party – so they sent him to work in a sugar factory. Then he and his friends began distributing anti-Nazi leaflets, and they built a transistor radio to get outside information about the war. This, of course, was illegal, and the Gestapo caught them and they were sent to Rothensee prison camp. They still used guillotines then, and every Monday that's all they heard: that blade dropping, severing heads above their ceiling floor. Then two weeks passed, and they were sent to Magdeburg and Halle, concentration camps, where they would remain, mostly, for the duration of the war.

I told her how one afternoon my grandfather's friend said he was going to try and escape. I'm going to try and escape, he said. But if I don't make it you can have my bike. So his friend told him where the bike was, and then he ran for the fence, and bullets went through his head and chest and arms and legs. I told her my grandfather turned to God and began to pray. He prayed he wouldn't die and that his pneumonia would go away. He asked God for help and to make him strong. Two years passed – then one day they let him go. They said he was sick and he probably wouldn't live much longer. So he left. He walked a few hours to where the bike was, and guess what? The bike was still there. Course he was in Germany, and his real home was in the Netherlands so it took a few days.

Then I told her that after the war he moved to Australia and became a minister and professor in sociology and religion. He met his wife, Ruth, and she told him to quit smoking and they had four children and one of them was my dad. I told her he lectured in universities all around the world, and he wrote fifteen books including one called *How God Hoodwinked Hitler*, and that after the war he never ate potatoes ever again. I said, Once you've been through hell, why would you ever go back? But then I told her if you knew him, really knew him, you'd know how funny he was too, how sometimes he would invite friends from the ministry or the university and serve them goon poured from expensive wine bottles. I told her that after you survive a war you're allowed to do anything. Then I told her that everything would be okay. I told her she'd find a job and that my migraines would go away and then I started doing my storm dance. I told her we were in the storm right now, but guess what happens after a storm? Then I did my rainbow dance and began moving her arms and legs so she did the rainbow dance too. Uh oh, I said, waving her arms from side to side. Looks like we got a rainbow in the room already! She told me to stop. She said she wasn't a rainbow, but I just made a confused face and apologized because I couldn't speak rainbow. Then I told her she was beautiful. I told her I loved her and that we just had to keep smiling. I told her things were hard right now but we would stop crying and things would look up; we just had to believe. Then I strung together a metaphor about Coke-A-Cola and how you could use it as a cleaning product. I told her even the terrible things could be beautiful if you looked at them right. I told her we were together because pneumonia had saved my grandfather's life.

She told me I was lucky. She said she never knew her grandparents but her mum had told her stories. She told me her grandpa killed himself in his garage one summer and her grandma overdosed on OxyContin the winter after. She told me her uncle used to beat her aunty, but then he got cancer and didn't want to wait. So he took a bunch of pills and passed out in the bathtub. But then something happened. His wife found him. They drove to emergency and his stomach was pumped. Behind curtains, she wept. Don't leave me. Don't leave me. And so she waited, holding his hand. She waited for him to wake. An hour passed and she began making deals with herself: if you let him wake he never broke my nose. If you let him wake he never touched alcohol. She found herself doing the thing we all do sometimes: she began praying to a God she didn't believe in to rearrange the past because she knew the only thing worse than actually remembering would be to remember it in the future, alone.

Six hours and he woke. I love you, she said. So much.

On the way home they held hands while they drove. And for a second in their kitchen she felt as if they were younger, maybe teenagers, momentarily blinded: as if their sum individual experiences hadn't resulted in them, but rather alternative and better versions of them. They went to bed projecting the future. They went to bed together, not alone. We'll make it work, she said. I promise. Except when she woke no one was there. The garage was closed and the car's engine was on; he was slumped over the wheel. There was no note. There were no good-byes. People fucking die, Maria said. And you know what? She was right.

***

Occasionally, after work, I would leave Redfern station and return to that street, that house, where everything had happened long ago. I would walk slowly and peer through the front window into our dining room that had transformed into a bedroom, and when the front door was open I'd see into the living room where all the furniture had been replaced, and then, for a second, I'd close my eyes and see myself and Maria and all the fragments of what we had said and done. I'd see those afternoons where she told me we had to be tough, and those evenings when she promised that the pain would pass and everything would be okay. I'd see the nights where she cried and I told her she was loved and she belonged and I promised she wasn't alone. And then, if I really tried, I'd see that morning, four months into the migraine, when I woke and felt no pain.

I got out of bed and felt no pain, and I brushed my teeth and felt no pain, and I showered and ate breakfast and felt no pain too. Maria was in the shower, and I shouted Maria! and then I opened the door and yelled, I'm back, baby! I'm back! and I shadow-boxed the air. Then I went downstairs and shadow-boxed the kitchen. Then I sat in my chair and shadow-boxed a pen and a piece of paper too.

When she came downstairs I flung my dick and balls in a 360 and told her Daddy was back. She told Daddy that our housemates were home and that Daddy should put his dick away. Daddy should also stop referring to himself as Daddy, she said, and then she smiled and told Daddy to take it easy. Remember what happened last time? Remember—but I was already outside, and the world looked different, or the world looked like how I remembered it, before the migraine, before I forgot.

That evening we sat in front of the TV and pretended, or no longer had to, to be a normal couple. We drank cheap wine and watched *Die Hard*, and every five minutes Maria kept asking if I was okay. I hadn't watched TV in so long, and I kept looking away out of habit, closing my eyes, then opening them, checking for the pain. Yeah, I'm okay, I would say, and then we would hold hands and kiss or laugh, or perhaps I made no expression at all; perhaps, in that moment, watching that Bruce Willis film, I felt utterly sedated, or happy, as if we were in a film of our own, a plot where the ending had already been decided, or maybe it's easier to say that wedged between her and Bruce Willis, I saw the attraction of never trying hard at anything ever again, of growing old together, fat together, but a pain-free fat, a comfortable fat that cushioned and protected, a fat that sounded a lot like love but wasn't love. In the past I had known those other loves: the love of a parent, the love of a friend, the love of a pet, the first love, the second love, the love of a stranger, but now, I knew, in that moment, I would settle for this new kind of love – so long as I wasn't in pain I would do all the terrible and boring things one was required to do to preserve this new kind of love.

But twenty minutes later, inevitably, it all fell apart. A metallic dulling. A shovel striking, but also grinding, electrical. Like lightning that doesn't go away. I closed my eyes, began clenching my jaw. Are you okay? Maria asked, again, but I just nodded, imitating the laugh I'd made only minutes before, imitating the smile of the characters I'd seen on the TV, imitating myself, my old self – just keep imitating your old self, I thought, walking to the bathroom, my hands in fists, shaking, and everything will be okay.

***

The migraine wasn't all sadness and pain: we played our games too. The first game we played was called *Water In The Whisky*, where we drank small amounts of our housemate's whisky and replaced it with water.

The second game was called *Swipe And Pray* – at this point my casual job, whose hours had been cut, left only enough for the bare necessities, and sometimes Maria's mum would load $20 on to her card as a surprise; at any rate, we would go for walks attempting to pay for what we called 'special treats' with money we did not know we had.

The third game we played was called *Aim And Piss*. One evening we returned home from an exhibition. We were drunk; we both needed to piss – in fact, we announced it, but instead of taking turns, we ran. I had a longer stride, but she had a head start, which meant we reached the bathroom door at the same time, shutting each other inside.

She sat first, pulled down her pants, released a strong flow of urine and, staring into my eyes, said, Oh, that's good. When I was younger I used to punch my bladder and this would, momentarily, send the piss away, but now, I knew, if I punched my bladder it would burst. So I looked at the sink. Don't you piss in the sink. Then I looked between her legs, and, at this, she opened them slightly and said, Don't you piss on my legs.

We pissed together for a long time, and later we would agree there was something special or even heroic about it, the way the two piss streams had become one, and from then on, when we were drunk, or if it was convenient, we would continue to play *Aim And Piss*, sometimes even reversing the roles, so that I would sit and she would squat over me; needless to say we both ended up, at various points, covered in each other's urine, which, if nothing else, proves that we were, if only for a little while, in love.

***

We lived with two girls: the taller one had been seeing her boyfriend for nearly two years. They were planning a trip to Bali, but had not yet committed because she was worried about what she called 'the culture shock'. He hasn't left Australia, she explained, and I don't know if he's ready. He's sort of funny around Asians.

The other housemate either did or did not have a boyfriend. In the beginning a swimmer would drop by, although over time his visits became less frequent, until he stopped coming altogether. At the same time a large, plastic dehumidifier materialized on one of the kitchen countertops, and in the evenings a vague humming haunted the kitchen as sweet potatoes, apples and pears dehydrated in the darkness. Fuck me, Maria said one night, as we crept downstairs to steal more whisky. That's the most depressing sound I've ever heard.

We thought our housemates were uptight, square, rude and anal, and they thought we were freeloaders, messy, loud and disrespectful, and so the house entered into a period of passive-aggressive note writing, labels and online messaging. For example the sugar was labelled as ****'s SUGAR, and the tea was labelled as *****'s TEA. One message, sent from a housemate in her room to me and Maria in our room, read: PLEASE DON'T USE MY SUGAR! GET A JOB IF YOU CAN'T AFFORD YOUR OWN SUGAR! And another read: PRETTY SURE SOMEONE USED MY TEA LAST NIGHT. NOT TRYING TO BE THE TEA POLICE BUT JUST SAYING!

In truth, we had been using their tea and sugar, though only slightly, but after the notes and especially after the messages, we began using their tea and sugar with wild abandon, because, as Maria said one night in a vague southern accent: Aah reckon, fuck they-em!

Call it pride. Call it cowardice. Call it stupidity – I never told my housemates about the migraine, not really; I suppose, when I moved in, I told them a half-truth: that my head had been hurting, but I wanted that room so badly – I'd been living at Toby's for three months by then, and I no longer wanted to impose. So I turned the pain into a joke. Message me your bank details, I might have said, laughing, I'll transfer the deposit when I can. Can't look at a phone right now. Killer headache. Big night on the piss!

But a month later I still had not told them; I guess it all just seemed so unbelievable, the pain, sure, but also the practicality of it all: not being able to look at messages, closing my eyes whenever I passed the TV in the living room, averting my gaze from the laptops playing movies in the kitchen. Besides, we were on pretty bad terms by then; beyond helping ourselves to their whisky, tea and sugar, I had failed to mention that Maria had permanently moved in.

One evening, Maria and I had a fight. There was yelling and shouting. A door slammed. We were either fighting because she was sick of taking care of me, or because I wanted her to get a job, or because we were broke, or because our housemates wanted her to move out, or because I didn't know how to explain to my housemates that I needed her, that I couldn't do whatever this was without her, that sometimes when I slept I only pretended to sleep, that I would wait for the moment that she, in her sleep, began to tremble and yell, and I would try to wake—

That night, after she left, I walked the streets of Darlington calling her name. I walked up and down Abercrombie Street, then Wilson Street. Eventually, I found her in the park. More yelling. Crying. Then silence. I got scared, I said. Of what? That you'd left.

For years after the migraine ended I would try and tell psychologists or friends or family about Maria and all that happened long ago – but, predictably, it would always come out wrong, or it would not come out at all – the specifics of what I wanted to say always felt beyond reach, beyond translation, and, mostly, it was all I could do to not burst into tears – at the pain, sure, but also at my inability to transform what I had always been able to transform: images into words, discomfort into paragraphs, the future into something tangible. I suppose all that was had been so coloured and marked by anger and terror that I felt incapable of seeing that there had been undeniable, heightened moments of beauty, or if not beauty then something close to beauty, perhaps awe, as well.

Like the time Maria announced we would start reading books together. She said she knew how much I loved books, so while I was blind she would be my eyes. Then she covered my eyes with her hands and said, Who's my little blind boy? I told her I didn't know, but it sure as hell wasn't me. I told her I was her blind man, the toughest blind man she'd ever seen. Then I told her if she was stowing any blind boys in the house she better get rid of them. Our housemates already wanted to kick her out, so the extra blind boys she was hiding should probably get out while they had the chance. Then I told her thank you. I told her I couldn't remember the last time I'd read, really read. A few weeks earlier I'd received Joe Brainard's *I Remember,* an unexpected gift from my friend Anthony in Chicago, and that day there'd been a moment, brief moment, when I thought the pain had gone, and so I'd picked up the book and begun to read; that first page, timidly, as if in hiding, but the second page, lavishly, indulgently, but twenty seconds later I couldn't, everything—It's okay, Maria said. I remember taking a breath, trying to compose myself. For a while, neither of us spoke, her hand making small circles on my back while I shook. I can't read, I said, finally. And no one knows why.

Know this: during those ten months, the pain never went away, not really. At certain hours of the day, and on a certain amount of drugs, it would dip, but the tension, the grinding, the electricity, the dulling, like a skull cut open, pierced or injected with lead was constant, and every time I believed that things had changed, that I could read or write or look in a mirror or glance at the price of food at the grocery store, the pain would return and hammer with such ferocity that I would hold my breath until I couldn't breathe, alternating between fury and apology, promising that I would not try again, that I knew my place, that if the pain would just go away I would not try for all those things I had done before.

***

One afternoon, we caught the ferry to Manly, and as we passed the Sydney Opera House, Harbour Bridge and Prime Minister's house I announced them as if I were a tour guide. You know, you're pretty shit at most things, Maria said. But the announcing! If you could just memorize a script, and tell stories – we might be in business, baby.

That evening, and the evenings thereafter, we stayed up late and she helped me learn one of my stories, line by line. It was the last story I'd written before the migraine came and I must have repeated it over a thousand times. Beyond exercising, there was little I could do that would not cause pain, and during the daytime, when she was out applying for jobs, or sleeping, I would take my pain pills and practise the pitch and practise the tone and practise the pace and practise the depth. I'd practise the parts where my voice went all raspy and I'd stare at the ceiling and pretend all that white space were my future and past and family and friends. Then I'd take another painkiller and pretend I could read and pretend I could write. I'd pretend I was better. The story began with, *I'd been known to do dumb things before*, and I'd say the story over and over until the story became a portal. I told myself all I had to do was remember that story. I'd had the pain for forty days and I knew it couldn't last much longer. I knew if I could just remember that story then everything would be okay.

This is, of course, a fiction, or not a fiction, but an attempt, a sketch, a version. Beyond the uncompromising fallibility of memory, and the unfathomable distances that a story must travel from event to memory to speech or page, we can never tell the whole story because truth, unlike people, cannot be isolated, and therein lies its beauty, its attraction – it dances from person to person, and even if we could, which we cannot, there are simply those stories that are not ours to tell.

An example: one night Maria told me about the first time she liked, really liked, someone. They were in year five, maybe six, and she was twelve years old. There was a boy in her class; sometimes they ate lunch together; she thought he was funny and cute. One day he asked to meet her behind the gymnasium after school. In English, she could barely concentrate. She kept wondering if he was going to kiss her. After school, she grabbed her bag; she checked her appearance, and then she found him behind the gymnasium. Hey, she said. Hey, he said. They started making out. But then something happened. She felt two hands on her shoulders, pushing her down, and then his knee connected with her thigh and she fell to the ground. There was a hand on her mouth; she tried to scream but it came out muffled. Get on your knees, he said. After it happened, he told her if she told anyone he would kill her. After it happened, she walked home and took a shower. She rinsed her mouth, washed the blood from her knee. Over dinner, her mum asked her what happened. I fell, she said.

That night I couldn't talk. I wanted to do something, anything – I wanted to do the impossible; I wanted to travel back in time, to help, to protect – but I couldn't. Instead, I began to shake. We held one another, and at some point I began to cry. It's okay, she said, running her hands through my hair. It's over now.

I remember the day Maria got a job, and that evening we went to a bar to celebrate. We ordered drinks and food we couldn't afford, and held hands beneath the table, and if you had seen us, then, our smiles, you would have almost thought we were happy, which, in that moment, we were. That night, on the walk home, I started telling her about Hazo and the hundreds of thousands of dollars she'd spent on the pokies in the last years of her life. I told her about all the cigarettes she smoked and how she was always putting down her dogs because they bit people and how, before she got married, she told Graham if he didn't ask to marry her she would join the Air Force. So Graham asked Hazo to marry him, but then Hazo said, I'll only marry you if you buy me a washing machine. I told her Hazo was a hero, and then I told her she was a hero too. I told her how proud of her I was, of us, with our jobs – but then, abruptly, she began slurring her words, and collapsed. On the grass, I kept saying her name; at first, in a whisper, but then not; I kept rubbing her shoulders, touching her head, asking, yelling, pleading, for her to wake. At some point, her eyes opened. Are you okay? I asked. She giggled. Sometimes I collapse, she said later, in the shower. If I get too stressed my body shuts down. What are you stressed about? I asked. I don't know, she said. Everything.

Maria's job hadn't worked out, and we decided, then, that the answer to all our problems was money. She said if we had more money we could afford more therapy and see more special doctors and we could even go on some dates too.

That afternoon, skateboarding to work, I saw a sign that announced Dymocks Bookstore was advertising a full-time sales role. For a long time I had wanted to work in a bookstore, although I had never been hired: I was too young, or I didn't have experience, or I didn't know the right people. But now, I thought, with a book published, if I could just get an interview and not look at a screen, if I could just take a few more painkillers and pretend to be normal, capable, if Maria could just help write my résumé and print my résumé, if I just kept my eyes closed on the train, and if I just smiled or pretended to smile – if I just went on pretending a little longer then maybe everything would be okay.

Let me look at you, Maria said, outside the store, straightening my tie. Several days earlier I had walked into Dymocks, eyes closed, cracked, trying to protect myself from the lights, but also from those books, their titles, those words that pierced my skull like bullets. I spoke, briefly, to that sales assistant and passed her my résumé, trying to match her enthusiasm, her smile; then I remember walking to the disabled bathroom and lying on the floor. How are you feeling? Maria asked. I nodded. You've got this, she said. I'll be right outside.

What happened next occurred quickly, and in blurs, and, even now, I don't know whether to view it comically or tragically, although in the end, I suppose, they are the same thing.

I took two painkillers and walked to the back of the store and asked the bookseller where I could find the manager. The bookseller asked if I had an interview. I nodded. Then the bookseller said the manager would be with me soon and told me to fill out a form. At first, absurdly, I protested. Do I have to? I mean, don't you

already have my résumé? It's store policy, he said, turning his back. So I glanced at the form and the world
grew smaller. Even now, it feels redundant trying to
describe it: grinding, like a piece of a metal being forced
into two. So I smiled and closed my eyes and wrote my
name and phone number and address and whatever else
they required that I can no longer remember, and when
I glanced again the writing was distributed unevenly
around the page. You can do this, I said, or thought, or I
travel back in time, now, and tell myself. You're okay.

When the manager arrived we shook hands and she
told me to follow her around the store. We walked past
the fiction and non-fiction and travel and memoir sections,
and when we arrived at the front of the store she asked
me what I did. I told her I was a writer. The codeine was
kicking in now and I told her when I was younger I'd
wanted to be a basketball player, but not any more. Now
I wanted to be a writer more than anything in the world.
Don't we all, she said. And what is it that you write? I
told her I wrote books, actually one book, and then, at
that moment, I glanced at a display titled: Dymocks
Favourites. There were books by Franz Kafka and
Haruki Murakami and Miranda July, and then there was
my book – a book in no way equal to its neighbours, a
book I still view with contempt, suspicion and regret,
but at the time it seemed so unbelievable all I could do
was point and smile. That, I said. I wrote that. The manager picked the book up, and read the title. Then she said
my name, and cross-checked it with the name I had
made barely legible on the form in her hand. What's it

about? Nothing, I said. Everything. The usual – pain and hope and love and regret.

At some point we went to her office and she asked what selling experience I had. I told her that I used to work in a phone store when I was nineteen. I told her I received the sales gun award for the first quarter of 2009, and that our team went to the Gold Coast, and the tele-communication company put us up in a hotel, and we all went skinny dipping at 6 a.m. Then I told her I was kidding. I told her that was just one example of the kind of humour I liked to use when selling my customers the things they didn't need. Then I told her I was kidding again. Everyone, I said, needs books.

Then we got into a lengthy discussion about what books were and what they meant, and about our favourite types of books too. She loved fantasy, or used to love fantasy; in the present she had little time to read, although when she was younger, when she had time for such things, she loved fantasy. I would just read, she said, and the whole afternoon would go away. Then I told her I didn't so much love genre as I loved authors, or sentences. I mentioned some of the authors that I liked, and I told her how much these books had meant to me, that when I had first read them they had changed my life. Then I told her about a camping trip I had been on when I was young. I'd helped my dad chop the wood, and then we'd made a fire, and I sat by the campsite copying out the first chapter from *Danny, the Champion of the World*. I told her how I'd shown my father, and how proud of me he had been, but how he had encouraged me to come up with my own stories, my own words. And so I wrote my first collection of short stories when I was eight. It was called *My Published Stories*. There was a story about a robot with a big mouth who swallowed a door. And a story about a boy who tells the reader he went to the circus and saw a clown juggling, but then says, April fools! Then there was the story about the clown who just liked reading books because they were good to read. Then I smiled and said, It shouldn't be too hard to sell books because even as a child I knew they were good to read. It was dumb, juvenile, but in that moment we both smiled, and I wanted to hug her, then, because I hadn't talked about literature in so long. Each time I had tried it had only brought pain, and so I had ignored it, banished it, pushed it away, but this, now, with her, even on the pain pills, felt *real*, a slice of life that I had forgotten, and I wanted to be part of it, to return – it was a pleasure to meet you, she said, finally. We will be in touch soon.

Around this time, we decided that every day we would go walking. And so, we walked, that first time, around the streets of Erskineville and pointed at houses. Maria became a successful Parisian fashion designer, and I became a miner, and we pretended we could buy and own whatever houses we wanted. We told stories where we made love in the kitchens and love in the spare rooms and love in the spare bathrooms. There were so many rooms to make love in, we reasoned, it seemed a shame for any place to be left out.

But the next day Maria said she wanted to do something different. She said we should get out, explore. So we walked to the train station, but there, outside, I stopped. I told her I couldn't go any further, and she knew that. I told her I couldn't look past the windows and I couldn't look at the lights, even in my peripheral vision. And then I began taking steps back. I told her I thought I could do it, but I couldn't do it. I told her the pain—I could already feel it, I—but Maria just took my hand. Hey, she said. Hey. You're okay. And then she asked if I trusted her. I nodded, and she told me to close my eyes. I've got you, she said, and then we began to walk. She guided me to the ticket machine and she bought two tickets, and then she guided me through the turnstile and asked where I wanted to go. I told her I didn't know. Then she said that in front of us was a map. She told me that all the stations were there, and all I had to do was point. So I pointed, blindly, and she giggled and said, Well, I guess we're going to the toilet. Then she guided my hand and we pointed again.

That morning, on the train to Fairfield, I sat against the window. For a while, we didn't talk. Then she squeezed my hand and whispered that we were strong. She whispered that so many other people would have given up by now, but not us. Then she whispered, Fuck everyone else. We don't need anyone. We've got us. I remember the way the light, behind closed eyes, flickered, the weight of her hand in mine, the sound of the train accelerating, slowing, then pulling out of the station. I remember the dull, constant thud inside my head – unpleasant, sure, but, in that moment, not horrific – or horrific but manageable. I remember leaving the station, walking around Fairfield, sharing falafel at an Iraqi restaurant, then her reading to me, out loud, from Miles Allinson's *Fever of Animals*. Then I remember my phone vibrated and Maria read the message that told me I didn't get the job. I told Maria it was okay. It was just a stupid idea anyway. Then I laughed and told her I had to go to the bathroom. She smiled and asked if I wanted to play Aim and Piss, but I just kept smiling and told her I'd be back. Then I got up from the table and walked, my vision blotting, clouding, towards the door. I remember stepping inside, fumbling with the lock and putting my hands on the wall. I shook, staring at the ground—I shook, breathing, or trying to breathe—I just wanted the pain to stop, or to go, or get out of my head. I just wanted, *needed*—I was so done with the boredom, that absurd, monotonous, terrifying sameness, and I just wanted to be new, or old, or anything other than—I just wanted to *change*. I pushed my nails into the flesh of my fingers and they bled and I doubled over, sobbing. I punched myself in the bladder and I punched myself again. I just wanted to *feel*, or to feel something different than what I knew. I had no control over my body and I just wanted control. I didn't want to hurt but if I had to, to hurt differently— I'd been hurting for so long and I needed a break, or at least for that hurt to be new. I put my hands around my throat; I squeezed, and then I punched myself again. At some point, I collapsed. I held my fingers in fists and lay there. I don't know for how long.

I now understand this: stories are miracles. We live and breathe inside them, and they live and breathe inside us, and we take all the mysterious and spectacular and impossible things that ever happened and they make us new. Throughout the migraine I tried, and failed, to write through the pain, and in the years that followed I tried to write around it, terrified to look at it dead on. The idea that, one day, I would travel through the fictions of my own mind seemed impossible, incredible, because I knew that if I wrote about the past I would relive it in the present and I would wake the monsters inside me and keep them alive.

But we have to – because the alternative is crippling – because monsters only live under beds when we choose to ignore them – because whole worlds illuminate when we turn on the light. I couldn't tell you the truth about Maria and me and all that happened even if I wanted to – I simply don't remember, not exactly, not accurately, and even if I could, which would be impossible, the truth would be so warped by codeine, pain, depression and despair, its edges so frayed that, were I to relive it, I am not sure I would recognize it at all.

And yet, we try, we must – we pick at fragments and assemble memories from the half-remembered past, and we put all those fictions together and call it our lives.

I have so many drafts of this story, so many edits, that if someone asked me what happened and in what order I would not know where to begin. Even now, as I write this, I feel my head throbbing, the outline of that remembered pain from all those years ago. But the difference, now, is that I am no longer scared, and in the process I learned how to tell the story where I picked myself off the floor and saved my own life.

So let us return to those places of horror and terror and let us whisper to ourselves that everything will be okay – because what I would give, now, to be a voice in my own head, then, a voice that cancelled out all the other voices, a voice that could see the future, that said: you are not useless or hopeless, that the pain would go away, that I would change and heal, and that one day I would even read train maps and menus and books again too. What I would have given to know that, one day, I would write again – perhaps not beautifully, or clearly like my heroes, but that I would, at least, be able to try.

Prayer

How do I stop telling this story? For years I tried to bury all that happened; I put on a brave face and told myself I was fine and mostly – although, perhaps not – I was good at hiding, at pretending everything was okay, but every now and then I would falter and tell someone how I really felt. Honestly, a friend told me one night, you just need to get the fuck over it. What happened to you was shitty, but now it's just, you know, depressing. It was the tail end of a bender, close to 6 a.m., that moment before the sun rose, and we were snorting someone's cocaine from her phone. No one cares, she said, finally, clearing one nostril and then the other. Not really. I remember, shortly after, stumbling home, occasionally running, then stopping, telling myself that she was right, that I would bury it, that I would put on a brave face and swallow all my sadness and try not to talk about it ever again.

But how do you do that? How do you take all that ever was and make it go away?

***

Each day, before work, I would pray, not to God but to myself, that my body would perform, that I would be able to sit in a chair, fill out my timesheet, look at my phone, at the work-issued iPad, at the pages I had saved that outlined the procedures we would follow so that no one would die. At some point I had discovered a website that claimed to cure chronic pain through movement, and after my prayers I would complete a thirty minute sequence of exercises: in the shower, under hot water, I would rotate my neck fifty times one way, and fifty times another, and when I returned to my room I would twist and contort and open and close my body in a sort of yoga/Pilates bastardization, in the way the pain-free model on the website had shown me.

And for a while, mostly, it worked. The pain stayed out of my head, moving instead to my neck, my shoulders, occasionally my back, always to my jaw. In the future this would become a major clue, but at the time this dancing pain was every bit as mysterious as it was debilitating, demoralizing. Sometimes, on the train, when I felt the pain returning, I would push my chin towards my neck as if I were choking myself, the way a mostly useless physio-therapist had shown me long ago. Other times, I would tell myself to breathe. But mostly, miraculously, at least during that first year, the pain came, but it also went, or the pain stayed out of my head, and I sat on the train making my announcements and opening doors, checking that no one had fallen between the gap, thinking about all the ways I was to prevent death and destruction and everything from going wrong.

At the start of a shift the booker-on would ask whether we were okay, and we would reply that, Yes, we were okay, which meant we were free from drugs and alcohol – because this was not what some of the old guards and drivers remembered as the Good Old Days, when management didn't have cameras and there were no phones or drug or alcohol tests, and a guard could enjoy a quiet six pack on the way to Waterfall, or deal a bit of heroin in between making their announcements, or at the very least burn a spliff under the full moon on the way to the sheds.

Sometimes I would even joke that I was more than okay, that I was ecstatic. I'd say, Oh, you better believe I'm ecstatic! which, given I'd found a job I could work, I was. And so we would sign on, receive our stopping patterns, and then head to the platforms to meet our trains, to relieve our co-workers, which in the beginning had been stressful, trying to recall which lines went where, though by the end had become second nature: the network and all of us inside it, humming beneath the same frequency, 1,500V.

Sometimes, in my guard's compartment, waiting to blow my whistle and depart, to close the doors so that we could return from those platforms that lay beneath Bondi

Junction, North Sydney and Central, I would sit and sketch scenes from those years I'd tried to remember – the words, until then, had been impossible, but I thought if I could just visualize, then witness those outlines I could, at the very least, give them titles and label whatever was inside me before throwing it, dramatically, in the bin.

What are you doing? station staff would ask, occasionally, but I would reply, Nothing, that I was waiting, and they would say, Aren't we all, and then we would have another conversation about how long we had until knock-off, or about the holidays we would go on nine months ahead, or about the strikes that were planned because drivers were working thirteen-day fortnights to ensure the network operated at all.

I suppose, I think now, I was trying to sort through the rubble, to compartmentalize my life, order it, something I'd never done, in the hopes that it might return to something vaguely identifiable, to something that made sense. By then I was able, with frequent breaks and barbaric neck manipulation and stretching, to read several pages of a book each day, and one afternoon waiting to depart Cronulla I read the following sentence from Kurt Vonnegut's *Palm Sunday*. 'The artist says, "I can do very little about the chaos around me, but at least I can reduce to perfect order this square of canvas, this piece of paper, this chunk of stone."'

Even so, those stories, early stories, on the backs of train diagrams, were nothing more than sketches, and as I attempted to flesh them out, to give them life, colour, I would think, or over-think, or stress about who would read those stories, and what would happen if they failed, and the back pain or shoulder pain or neck pain or headaches or migraines would, occasionally, return, and each time I would renounce writing all over again, preferring, instead, to think that I was a failure, that there was something fundamentally wrong not only with me, but with the work.

But for the most part this was a period of calm. I learned to limit myself to writing ten minutes per day, and when the pain returned I would sit and breathe and push my thumbs into the muscles where the Healer said the pain had lived. Overall, I felt myself getting better, becoming less useless, more self-reliant. I knew I would never be a writer, and I knew I would never work an office job or be able to look at a computer, but I no longer cared. I had the trains, and it was a relief to know my role, to be given a daily plan, to surrender to something larger than myself. In the beginning I resisted, but later I grew to love the repetitive rituals that became everyday life: swiping in, filling out the timesheets, blowing whistles, making announcements, opening and closing doors, waking at two or three or four in the morning, watching the sun come up over Waterfall, Penrith or Hornsby. It was, at the right hours and in certain lights, romantic, the way writing or literature or movies or the fictions inside my head had once promised to be.

See this cunt up here? a driver said, one afternoon, pointing at the signaller standing in the rain. I was riding up
front and we were travelling that now-defunct route
between Clyde and Carlingford, in one of those now-
defunct S set trains, smoking cigarettes and listening to
jazz from a transistor radio with our feet on the dash.
Poor cunt. He's been here for years. First time I saw him
I gave him the horn because I needed the signal and
thought he was sleeping. Like, wake up, cunt. You know?
Eventually, I wondered if the cunt was taking the piss.
So I yelled, What's the hold-up? and he yelled, Nothing.
Then I yelled, Well, raise your fucking arm and give us
the signal. And he yelled back, I am. Then he took out
his arm, which stopped at the shoulder, and waved it in
the rain. The mad cunt was grinning, just waving his
stump in the air, he said. As we passed, they yelled and
laughed at one another through the window.

But if you really want to know about the trains and the
guards and the lives we led, then, I would tell you about
those conversations that happened without words, or
few words, in passing. Often, at Glenfield, two trains
would depart at the same time, and as our trains picked
up speed the other guard and I would hang out of our
respective doors, confirming the proceed signal, checking no one had fallen between train and track, that kids
had not leapt from prams, that lovers had not pushed
one another on to the rails, and as we prepared to close

our own doors we would give each other the nod. I loved those nods, and after a while I even gave them a name – the Transport Nod. I would nod at my fellow transport workers going down escalators, passing in corridors and on platforms while waiting for trains. I would nod at fellow guards when I wasn't on duty, taking the train to various chiropractic, optometrist and neurological appointments. You give 'em the nod today? my brother would ask, as we spoke on my burner, and I would say, Oh, they got their nods. That's my guy, he would say. At Christmas, you can even make it festive. Call 'em egg nods. That's my guy, I would reply. There he is.

I remember, one afternoon, my last train was cancelled so I decided to take myself to the beach. Technically, I was still working, but I knew if I kept my head down, didn't report, I could slip away. So I hopped a train to Bondi Junction. But then, walking to the bus, I realized that if I tapped on using my Opal card they would know where I was. So instead, I waited, patiently, and when it was my turn I lowered my train-issued speed dealer sunglasses, said, Mate, and dropped a Transport Nod so violent I nearly fell over. It's hard to say whether it worked; in the end, I didn't turn around, just walked to the back of the bus and tried to conceal my smile, that smile that was still foreign to me, the one that I had lost years earlier when I couldn't ride a bus or a train, when I couldn't write, when I couldn't do much of anything at all.

Another day, sitting in the break room with my eyes closed, occasionally opening them to stare at the wall, this guard said, Let me give advice. Don't waste time on the fucking. You know? The whore. Dick. Pussy. Keep nose clean. Head down. Maybe in five years you own house. Then you already have the fucking. You think joking? The world is, how you say, fucking for you. Everything getting too hot. Oceans coming. Animals dead. Where the jobs? I tell you: don't fuck this up. He was fifty or sixty years old. His smile reminded me of the desert. I never learned his name. I never learned anyone's name – except Bruce.

Bruce was eighty-four years old and had come to the job out of obligation, rather than necessity, though it would be some time before I figured out what that meant.

Sometimes, in the break rooms, we would talk about Bruce and how he'd failed his practical exam three times because he kept falling asleep in the guard compartment, or about his oversized bag that he carried on his back with all the printouts of every rule in existence, and all the stopping patterns, and everything else that the guards carried around before the internet and iPads, those technologies that Bruce did not care for and did not know how to work. Shouldn't he be retired by now? a guard asked one afternoon. You know, a house in the country. Wife. Couple of dogs. Maybe a veggie patch?

Around this time, I began to see a girl from Brisbane. We were old friends; she was a musician, and her eyes reminded me of those fires that can be seen from space – intense, mesmerizing; they stared all the way into your soul. We would fly between Sydney and Brisbane, visiting one another, drinking dry Prosecco and smoking cigarettes and listening to the Go-Betweens – although, more often, we were apart. And so we would talk on the telephone about the possums that had moved into her parents' roof, and the fruit her mother fed them; about her father who liked to say, I'm here for a good time not a long time! before pouring the latest batch of homebrew into our glasses; about my grandmother who we couldn't call grandmother, but Hazo, who told her soon-to-be husband, Graham, that if he did not marry her she would join the Air Force, and when he did ask her she replied matter-of-factly, Only if you buy me a washing machine, but also about Brisbane itself – the tunnels that existed or presumably existed between certain nightclubs in the valley, or about the Lesbian Vampire Killer who seduced a man at The Beat then stabbed him to death on the banks of the Brisbane river, almost decapitating him and drinking his blood.

Invariably, though, our conversations always returned to Bruce, who had become a source of fascination to us, and I would fill her in on the phone calls I had overheard, demonstrating the way he had been yelling, waving his hands, negotiating some deal or another, attempting to buy land or a car. I love him, she would say. He's such a *mystery*. Such a *bloody* battler.

I suppose we all came to the job for our own reasons – some had been schoolteachers, mechanics, pilots, doctors; others had worked in security, in the army, in corporate finance. I remember, one morning during train school our teacher asked us why we had joined the railway. I was sick of busting my arse for fuck-all pay; I was sick of doing overtime for free; I was sick of sitting at a desk; I hated my boss; people treated me like shit; I felt stuck; I was sick of the commute, of patients, of co-workers; I wanted change, more money, more holidays; I wanted something different, to be better, stable; I wanted regularity, structure; I wanted to belong – but Bruce had been retired for fifteen years before joining the railway; the way I heard it, he didn't need the money, and while everyone else watched the footy I watched, happily, his eyes widen behind those thick glasses as he spat and barked orders to strangers on Gumtree down his phone. I don't get it, I told her one evening. I heard he was an accountant, that he's rich. Maybe he's just lonely? she said. Maybe he just wants to stay young?

Another morning, waiting for my train on the platform, Bruce arrived, looking dishevelled, angry. The bastards are trying to get rid of me, he said. They're saying I'm not fit for the job. Who's saying that? Who do you think? Those fat, useless cunts upstairs. In the end, Bruce had given the driver the all-clear when the light was still red and they didn't have the road. But it wasn't my fault, he said. It was raining, peak hour and the station staff gave me the flag, right of way. They think I'm a liability. But they're the liability! Liable to have a fat fucking heart attack – the cunts. We laughed, then, but as my train came he said, I'm going to fight them. I don't care what they say. I can't lose this job. My wife will kill me.

So he has a wife, she said on the phone that evening – now that is interesting. For a while we speculated, wildly, as to the reasons Bruce's wife might kill him: he had gambling debts; the job meant he had to stay off the booze; he was terminally ill and trying to secure, for his wife, a pension, but in the end all we spoke about was the new car I'd heard him buying, and the couches he had upgraded. I told her I'd watched him dial the number, and when the person answered he said, The name's Bruce – talk to me about your couches. God, she said. How *brazen*. Now there's a man who gets shit done.

Sometimes, in the evenings, she would show me the songs that she had recorded but had not yet shown others, and in the days apart, on the train, secretly, obsessively, I would play them over and over, writing, pleasurably for ten, then twenty minutes, those monotonous sentences and terrible poems that I vowed never to show anyone.

And now, all these years later, I realize that I never said thank you: because she showed me that it was okay, or more than okay, to create; because she listened to my writing and did not laugh; because, unknowingly, through her work, she gave me permission; she showed me how important it was, is, to try. So if you're reading this now:

Thank you, from the bottom of my heart.

Mostly, though, we just had fun. One evening, we went to the strip club where we met the Albanian who could suck his own dick. Another night she picked me up from the airport and told me she had a surprise. This is my favourite place in Brisbane, she said, as we sat drinking XXXX pints at the Brook Hotel in Michelton. It was karaoke night, and there were ten people, maybe fifteen, mostly labourers in high-vis, men over fifty, drinking rum and Cokes. We sat in silence, holding hands under the table, while men sang 'Black Betty', then 'Highway to Hell' to that mostly empty, partially lit room. At some point, a man in a wheelchair placed two rum and Cokes on the stage, drank two more, then whispered Celine Dion's 'My Heart Will Go On' into the microphone as if it were a poem. Jesus Christ, she whispered, one hand on her heart, the other squeezing my hand with an intensity that I could not hope to replicate now, but were I to try, I would say that I wanted that moment, to know it forever.

Early on, we decided that our relationship would be open – we lived in separate cities; we were happy; why complicate things? The rules, we agreed, were that when we were together, we were together, and when we were apart, we practised safe sex, but one night in Brisbane I went home with someone else. The following morning we spoke on the phone. Did you at least wear a condom? No, I said. What the fuck is wrong with you? I told her I didn't know. I felt stupid, embarrassed; I still do. I guess I always prided myself on having a moral compass, being fiercely loyal, having a certain amount of integrity. Even now, years later, it leaves a bad taste in my mouth – a deep discomfort knowing that I wasn't the man I thought I was. I apologized, or tried to apologize. Then I apologized again. I told her I was sorry. I didn't know why I did it. Yes, you do, she said. Because you were fucked up, and wanted to fuck and you don't think about anyone but yourself. She hung up, then, and I spent the better part of the afternoon writing her a letter. That evening, a few of her friends were playing at The Zoo, and she agreed to meet me, and when she arrived I felt so pathetic I struggled to meet her eye, but after a few seconds our stares dissolved and she put her hand on my shoulder and said, God, you're a fucking idiot.

Things, I suppose, returned to normal after that, or

we pretended they did, although we both knew the trust had been broken, and in my experience it is almost always impossible to return from something like that. Then a few months passed and we stopped seeing one another. She began to see someone else, and I did too, and three months later I did the same thing to my next partner, and everything turned to hell.

How could I be so selfish? Even now, I have no words for that next story, or I have millions of words for that person but none of those words for you, and when I look back, now, on that sentence – *I did the same thing to my next partner* – I see two people in love, then not in love, and I break. I break because I'm disappointed in myself and because it's sad and tragic and bullshit: the way we grow up to become the things we despised, how we hurt one another, the way I hurt her, and I am still trying to understand how I could have been so cruel. In many ways you don't need to know that story because it's a story you already know – I was a piece of shit; I fucked someone; I lied.

Not long after, the pain returned. At first, I wasn't scared, or I was, but I tried not to admit it, show it – I had my routine, my stretches; I knew what to do. But in the days that followed the pain was still there, and it was all

I could do to make announcements before commencing another round of stretches where I pressed my fingers and thumbs hard into my neck, into those homes where the Healer had told me the headaches lived. But the stretching and manipulating no longer worked, and during lunch breaks I would disappear to that other, quiet break room with the couches and lights turned off, or if people were talking, I would go to the bathroom and sit on one of the toilets and try to meditate, ignoring or trying to ignore the people pissing and shitting around me. Eventually, during my breaks, I simply returned to that park behind Central and did what I had done throughout the initial migraine: push-ups and sit-ups in the grass.

But things were not improving. One morning, returning from Richmond to the city after night shift, I was sitting downstairs in a deserted carriage with my eyes closed when a guy boarded the train and sat down in front of me. He was drinking a beer and talking to himself when, suddenly, he turned around and started talking to me. Any good? The job? You get free transport and shit? Yeah, I said. Fuck, that's pretty sweet. For a while he looked out the window, then I asked, How about you? What's up with you? I just finished fucking labouring – I hate that shit, but it keeps me out of trouble. Got the afternoon off so I thought I'd treat myself, he said, grinning, holding up his beer. You gotta treat yourself, I said. That's step one. Fuck yeah, bro, he said. Then he reached into his bag and said, You want one? I would, I replied, but then pointed to the cameras. Motherfuckers are always watching, bro. I nodded. Naa, it's good though, he said. You're being good. I'm trying to be good too. But it's hard, bro. Not having money and motherfuckers always giving you shit. Telling you you're not good enough, or you're useless – but fuck that shit, I'm strong. Then he took a long sip of beer and said, Wait, you're not gonna arrest me or nothing? That's not my job, I said. I just open and close doors, do the announcements, but I wouldn't arrest you even if I could. I like you, bro, he said. I told him I liked him too. For a while, neither of us said anything, but then he said, You know, I like myself too, bro. I mean, I got a big heart – but depression is real, bro. I never been to a doctor or nothing, bro, but I know I'm feeling down. I *know* I'm feeling down. I got my kids and my wife. She's bogan as hell, but she's a good woman. Good family. She's strong. She keeps telling me I'm on the meth, bro, but fuck that. I'm not on the meth. She keeps telling me I'm getting skinny 'cause of the meth, but if I was on the meth I'd be an Aussie, bro. I'd be a skinny cunt like you, bro. But I'm so stressed, bro. I got this friend who's in jail. She was on the meth, bro, and now she's fucked. But I'm not fucked. I gotta be strong for my family. I could go back to Auckland, but I'm not running out on my family, bro, fuck that. I gotta be strong. But it's so hard. I could count the people on my hands and toes who killed themselves. It's no joke, bro. Especially nowadays, bro. But, naa, I'm strong, bro. I'm strong. I know you're strong, I said. I gotta be strong, bro. You're strong, I said. How do you know? Because I know. You're strong too, bro. We're strong, I said. We're strong, he said. We gotta be. We're strong.

One afternoon Dad called me on the train and asked how I was and I told him not good and then I said, One second, and did an announcement. Then I told him I was stupid and pathetic and I'd fucked up and she would never forgive me and I was the dumbest person in the world. I told him I felt nervous and scared and I couldn't sleep and the pain had come back and my life was just one fuck-up after another and I deserved to be hated and I deserved everything that was coming for me and I deserved to be alone. Everything had been going so well, but now everything hurt and I would probably get fired because I couldn't even look at my roster on the work computer in the break room. I had to ask the booker-on to print the roster and I had made a joke about being allergic to computers, but soon they would know. They would know I was useless and they would know I was a failure and then I said, One second, and did another announcement. Then Dad said, You're not useless or a failure, Oliver, and I took a few breaths and said, I'm just in pain, Dad. So much pain. I told him how I'd gone to another headache doctor in Sydney who'd pushed on the muscles in my neck and told me nothing was wrong, and about the doctor who refused to give me a referral for the government's chronic pain management plan. I'd sat in his office and told him my whole stupid, sad, fucking, boring story and he'd just cut me off and said, Nope. I'm not giving you a referral, and I asked why and he said, I've never heard of anyone getting pain from a computer. Then he laughed and said, Try another doctor, buddy. I told Dad I almost hit him, or I wanted to. I told him about all the money I had spent on the kinesiologist and all the money I had spent on the acupuncturist and all the money I had spent on the lady who was teaching me how to sit and walk again. She taught something called the Alexander Technique, and I would go to her house in Rozelle and she would rearrange my body so that my spine was like a child's again. She said that when we grew up we became stiff and imbalanced but when we were children we were pure. She told me she used to be a ceramicist, but then she developed chronic pain so horrific she couldn't lean over the wheel and she couldn't get out of bed. But then she cured herself with the Alexander Technique and started teaching it too. I told Dad how kind she was, and how sometimes when I left I would be pain-free for thirty minutes, but then I would ride the bus home and the pain would come back. I told Dad each day I was trying to think child thoughts, that I was trying to laugh, to be different, to be pure, but I couldn't; it was so hard. And then I told Dad I was sorry; I had to go. I wasn't meant to be on my phone; I had a job to do. Then I apologized again and told him he didn't have to worry; I didn't mean to be dramatic—

Oliver, Dad said. Take a breath. I promise we're going

to figure this out. Okay? Okay, I said. Okay? Okay, I said, again, my voice cracking.

I think it might be a good idea to see another psychologist, Mum said that night over the phone, but I told her, Fuck psychologists. They were bullshit. I was so *sick* of people pretending they could help. I told her you just sat in their chairs and told them your pain and they nodded and took your money, but they never listened, not really. I told her the first guy I'd seen, years earlier, couldn't even look me in the eye. He had these bloodshot eyes and he smelled of piss and he kept shifting in his chair and staring at the clock while I tried to tell him my whole stupid, boring story. I told him I didn't know how much longer I could do it, that I'd had the pain for nine months, that I needed help, that every day—but then I shut up and promised myself I wouldn't cry. I promised myself I would cry later, but not in front of him. So I held my breath and stared at the ground and pressed my nails into my skin. I tried to clear my head, to think of something, anything, a joke, but then I smiled because I knew we were the joke. We were the hungover psychologist and the broken writer and I laughed because we were just two more clichéd characters from some terrible novel. Then I looked up and saw the food stains on his shirt and I knew he didn't care and the whole world didn't care and I tried to swallow it all down. I tried to put on a brave face and I tried to be normal, but I couldn't. This guy couldn't even take care of himself, I told Mum, finally, so how could he take care of anyone else?

Mum told me she didn't know.

Then I told her about the psychologist in the green dress. I told her how she invited me into her office and pointed at a chair and told me to sit, but I couldn't sit, not without painkillers, not really – so I told her I preferred to stand. And then I told her my stupid, sad story too. I told her I didn't even care about writing any more; I just wanted to be normal. I told her I just wanted the pain to go away. I told her so long as the pain left and I could walk under supermarket lights and look at screens, I would do anything. I would stock shelves at Coles or I would work the tills at McDonald's like I used to or I would work at Optus again. I didn't care, I said, honestly. I just wanted to work, to feel useful. And for a while, it almost seemed like she'd been listening. She'd been smiling and nodding and making concerned faces, and it almost seemed like I'd been heard. At the end she even leant forward and told me she could help. She said she recognized a lot of herself in me – that years earlier she'd been suffering from the same affliction. And, for a moment, I couldn't even talk. I wondered if she'd had migraines? If she had fixed them? I wondered if she had been a writer too? But then she said, Before I was a psychologist, I had problems with motivation. And then she told me how she had woken each morning and stared at the ceiling in her own bed, and about how useless she'd felt. But then, one day, she said, I started making lists. Lists! I told Mum. All she had to do was *listen*. Why couldn't she even do that?

Mum told me she didn't know that either.

Then I asked Mum if things would get better. Things had been going so well for so long, but now things had become much worse. I told her I was trying to keep it together, that mostly I was able to walk around with a smile on my face; I told her about my Transport Nods, how I'd nod and smile at the driver every time we changed ends, how one of us would ask, How ya going, mate? and the other would grin and say, Another day in paradise – but sometimes I couldn't help it, sometimes I would make it to my guard's compartment, close the door and—

I'm not going to do anything, I said, finally, not like— I just—I'm trying to be kind to myself, but it's—it's just hard. I keep telling myself what you told me, That it's not going to be like last time, but it's exactly like last time, it's—

Oliver, Mum said. Your father is here and I am here, and what you're going through I can't even begin to imagine, but we are here and we love you. We—Hi Oliver, Dad said. Hi Dad, I said, sobbing, though trying not to. I'm sorry we didn't get to talk longer on the train today – it sounds like you're having a pretty rough time of it at the moment. Yeah, I said, not a lot of fun. Is there anything we can do? I don't know, I said. Do you want me to come thump those arsehole, bullshit psychologists? Dave! Mum said. Well, Dad said. They sound like a bunch of arseholes in need of a good thumping! Maybe, I said, laughing, then crying again, wiping my eyes. You just tell us what you need, Dad said. Do you need money? No, I said, for once, at least, I have that. Do you need us to book your appointments? No, I said. My housemates are helping with that. I just—and then I told them they had already done so much. They had done more than anyone else. They had *listened.* I told them how that afternoon I had actually gone and seen another psychologist. I was just feeling so low and so down, and a friend had recommended her, and she could squeeze me in. I told her the pain would come and the pain would go, and that I couldn't control it, that some days I would be fine, more than fine, ecstatic, but that other days the pain would return and I would slide into a depression so deep I could not see my way out. I told her I felt like a rat in an experiment, a rat made to drink water – sometimes the water was normal but other times the water shocked with an electricity so violent that I would swear never to drink it again, but then I would see everyone else drinking water and I would wonder why I couldn't do that too. I told her I just wanted to drink the water. Sometimes I could, but mostly I couldn't and I never knew when. I told her I just wanted to know why. It had been years since I'd had the initial migraine, but even now, right then, the pain had returned and I couldn't read or write or—I told her I was sick of being an experiment, that I just wanted answers, someone to help. Then I asked her if she could help. I asked if she'd ever heard of anything like this before and then I told her please. I said, Please, I would just really appreciate it if you could help, and she just smiled and told me she'd seen it all before. Then she got out a piece of paper and a pen and told me to rewrite negative self-thoughts as positive self-thoughts. I asked her what she meant. She said, Well, you could rewrite *I am worthless* as *I am special*; *I am alone* as *I am loved*; *I am useless* as *I am capable*. And then she sat back and pushed the pen and paper towards me and told me to try. I told Mum and Dad I just got up and left, then – because I knew she was just the same as everyone else – full of bullshit just like the whole world was full of bullshit. I told them it was like I was eight years old, and everyone was playing pretend.

I'm not sure what was said after that; for the most part, my parents just consoled me while I cried. Eventually, we spoke about exercise, a possible return to Brisbane, to the Brisbane headache doctor again. I told them I was sorry: for making them worry, for being weak, a burden—but Mum just said, You call us whenever you need. We love you. We got through this once, and we will get through it again—and Oliver, Dad said. I promise it gets better. How do you know? I asked. Because I know, Dad said. Because you are my son – and we are stubborn and we are strong and we will get through this together.

In many ways I wish this story ended here, but it does not end here, cannot end here, because this story ends a different way.

Around then, Bruce stopped coming to work, but one afternoon I heard people talking. Poor bastard, one of them said. He didn't even need the money. His latest wife just wanted him out of the house. Then someone else said his first marriage hadn't worked out. Married for twenty years, then she took up with someone else. Years passed. He tried to meet a few people, but the bloke's seventy-five, and barely uses a phone. So he ordered a bride from Thailand. Then a few months later the real husband flew over and they disappeared. So he ordered another, but the same thing happened. He said Bruce had told him he was on his third wife in less than a year. At first, she wanted a bigger deck. So he built a bigger deck. Then she wanted a bigger bathroom. So Bruce knocked down a wall and extended the bathroom. Eventually, she told him to get a job. She told him she wanted her own space. She found him annoying; his voice, she said, was stupid. Besides, he couldn't just drink coffee and read the newspaper and sit around the house. So, through some miracle, he got a job here. All those couches he was buying, all those cars he was trading in were just to make her happy. But the other day he returned home, and she'd left.

More than five decades between us, only a handful of conversations, and yet sometimes, absurdly, I felt like I knew him. Not in temperament, but in stature, in form. His gait, the way he stooped, reminded me, at certain hours, of Graham, my mother's father, this man who I recall, now, only in images, in stills – this man who at first light is wearing dark green gumboots, frozen mid-step between his dam and the house, holding a bucket of feed for his chickens and ducks; this man who is at the beach in a bright red jumper smiling, childlike, into the depths of a rock pool; this man who is hooked up to a ventilator, trying, but failing, to say goodbye.

Sometimes, when we spoke about Bruce, and afterwards when I thought about Graham, I was reminded of Hazo, and those times during the initial migraine when I had tried to travel to *the before,* and when it had become too difficult to insert myself into my own memories, I had tried, as a last-ditch attempt, to remember, then place myself inside the Hazo stories of my uncle Tim and Uncle Steve and Aunty Jo and Mother. But I could not. Those doorways, I suppose, had sealed, and instead I lay there, praying, oscillating between numbness and despair, trying to picture them, their outline, which represented a sort of beacon, but being unable to – only able to remember that she had smoked, indulgently, and that he had been hard working, and kind.

But in an essay, which is not real life, I, the author, who is not the character, can rearrange text and insert memories that did not happen; I can play with space and time. For example, I can invent a scene where Maria squeezes

Oliver's hand on a train to Fairfield and tells him that they are strong, and I can conceive of worlds where boys named Dean have the courage to speak up, to say, even cryptically, that their parents are arseholes, that their dad's beat them, that something is wrong.

But other times, in the dead of the night, the truth of a story slaps so hard that I recoil and shudder; I shiver. Because no matter how many drafts I write where I try to save old men from heartbreak and boys and girls from themselves, from pain – I can't.

Here's the truth: writing these sentences hurt. Not in the way they used to, not physically, with a pounding or grinding or burning, but psychologically – beyond the trips or attempted trips down memory lane, I simply don't know how to translate all that happened, all that is untranslatable, and it aches.

So why do you do it? Sam asks, after another year goes by and I'm still working on the book. You'll think it's sappy, I say. Or worse – stupid. Try me, he says. Because I made prayers to myself all those years ago, and I'm trying to answer them with this book.

Horror

Listen: I'm trying, now, to remember, to isolate, to illuminate certain memories, to write with more restraint,
less emotion, but the book, the essay, this essay, the
format, the freedom, scares me – even now, I feel my
head, my neck, waking, firing: because the memory of it
hurts; because no one shows you how to do this; no one
shows you how to wake the monsters of the past, how
to keep the paragraphs short, how to create gaps, blank
space, places to breathe.

One morning, before work, I decided I would produce a long story. In the shower, I completed my neck
rotations, and after towelling off I looked in the mirror and announced it, solemnly, as if it were a death
sentence. For months, I had been writing, or trying to
write, those short stories that were hardly stories at
all, that appeared, at least in my mind, more as windows, but now, I thought, with a certain amount of
anxiety, although smiling at the inevitability of the
metaphor, I would try to build a house.

But at work, I could not do it. I wrote terrible sentence after terrible sentence, unable to connect them, and after some time I realized that I no longer knew how. I sat, for a while, in despair, dramatically, silently bemoaning, again, the loss of an identity, then barraging myself with the usual – that I was useless, that I would never write again – when, suddenly, I recalled being a child with my father, and copying out that first chapter from *Danny, the Champion of the World*. Then, in that moment directly after, I decided to reproduce the story that Maria had helped me memorize all those years ago. I thought if I reproduced that last, although admittedly average, story I had written before the pain I might pick up where I left off and remember how to write, and even, absurdly, who I was again too.

The work took longer than expected – writing beyond the length of a paragraph terrified me, and I kept pausing, assuring myself I was okay, then proceeding, cautiously, only to pause once more, watching, with a mixture of curiosity and fear as certain memories surfaced from long ago – Maria's face smiling, concentrating as she showed me how to cook a chickpea eggplant curry; her tears when she asked why men had done the things men do; the way she held me that night after we received the text message from Dymocks Bookstore, and she told me I worried too much, and she grabbed my hand and placed it to her cheek and told me to come upstairs, and we pushed our bed against the wall, and she explained that in a previous life she had been a dancer, a very good dancer, a dancer who danced all the bad things away, and she turned off the light and pressed play to Debussy's *Clair de Lune,* and we danced slowly, together, in our bedroom, and she said, One day, when this is all over, when you are better, you're going to write about this, us, and we will all just be a story.

***

What'cha writing? It was my mate who had told me about the microwave, leaning over my shoulder. Oh, nothing, I said. Just a story. Looks intense! he replied. The way you were gripping that pen, mamma mia – is it horror? I love horror, and then he proceeded to tell me his own horror story, how a few days earlier he'd nearly broken his neck on the BMX track at Castle Hill. Yeah, he said, it was pretty much fucking bullshit. Couple days ago I invested in a $200 BMX bike from Kmart. Went to Kmart for some undies, left with a bike. You know how it is. So then I had a day off and thought – let's take this bad girl to the track. That's the BMX track for those playing at home. So there I was, out there, lapping, getting some pretty sweet air, when my cleats locked into the pedal. Fucking ate shit. Told you it was bullshit. Your cleats? I asked. Well, he said. I had soccer after. Anyway, tell me about your story – is it horror? Can I read it?

I liked Microwave. He had a certain zip to him, an eccentricity that reminded me of childhood. I don't know if it's horror, I said. I guess there are some scary parts. You can read it, but I'm warning you, it's not very good: it jumps around in time; the introduction takes too long—Jeez, Microwave said. Who invited Negative Norman! I laughed, then, and passed him the story.

But what is horror, and how do we talk about it? After ten months, Maria and I began to fall apart. At first, it was crying: heaving, inconsolable crying. What's wrong? I would ask, holding her, stroking her hair, but she would just say, You wouldn't understand, that I couldn't know, shouldn't know. Then, later, it would be my turn. Baby, she would say. It's okay. Everything is going to be okay.

You're going to leave me, she said, one evening, sobbing, locking herself in the bathroom with a knife. I'm not, I said. I promise. Please. Don't forget who I am, she said. Maria, I pleaded. Please. Don't. Don't forget you need me, she said. Don't forget without me you can't see. You can't do anything without me. Don't forget that. For a while, neither of us spoke. Then she said, If you leave me I'll kill myself. Don't say that, please, I said. Why not? It's the truth.

For years, I have wrestled with this story, taking the few parts I remember and inventing or guessing or borrowing or approximating the many parts that I don't, trying to make sense of it, because it haunts me, this not understanding, this inability to recall, this push and pull between needing to tell my story and not being able to and telling another story that isn't my own.

Not long after, Maria moved out. This wasn't a break-up, but we needed space, and while I was terrified, I was also relieved. For the next few weeks, everything was fine; she found a job, and I upped my pain medication; we saw each other a few times per week, and while each day I felt less and less, I almost welcomed it, the noth-ingness of it, the way I learned or almost forgot how to cry.

Although perhaps everything was not fine; perhaps this was a break up and perhaps she was hurting; per-haps she just wanted someone to be there, to listen; perhaps, all that time, I knew the very definition of what it meant to cry.

Horror is living and breathing within the pages of a false reality for five years trying to explain a truth that cannot be remembered and even if one could remember it would hurt too much to tell. Horror is the impossibil-ity of story, of knowing that even if we could bear it the story would only ever be *our* truth, which is never the whole story, which is never enough.

Horror, I think, now, is never being enough.

One afternoon, I received a text message. Siri was no longer working; I had work in a few hours, and I knew if I looked at the phone the pain would become unbear-able, so I tried to look at it out of my periphery; I kept glancing at it, trying to make it out. Eventually, I saw it was from Maria, and I made out one of the words. Then another. Then I glanced at it dead on. I remember the world slowing, a searing hotness in my chest, followed by an impossible stuckness that made it hard to breathe, to move. And then, the whole world, moving: my lungs moving and my chest moving and my legs moving and my feet moving and hands moving and then I was calling. I was outside and I was calling and pacing and calling and pacing and calling and calling and then I was running. I was running and calling and running and calling and running and running and running and then I was praying. I was praying that she was at work and this was a joke and that no one was going to die. I was praying for once, please, to make us strong. Then I was calling and running and praying and calling and running and Maria was answering. I was saying, Maria. Please. Where are you? I love you, and, Maria. I'm coming. Just. Please. Hold on. But Maria was saying she didn't want to hold on. She was saying she was at work and she was going to hang up and there was nothing I could do. So then I was begging. I was running and begging and running and begging and yelling and pleading for her to keep talking. I was saying, I know you're hurting right now; I am too, but the world is good; I promise—Maria just listen to me I promise it's good and we can figure this out and we can find another house and I can take more pain pills and we can be there for each other and we can be like a little family again. But Maria wasn't saying anything because Maria was hanging up. So then I was calling and running and calling and running and then I was just running and running and running and running because Maria had turned off her phone.

By the time I reached St Peters I could no longer breathe. She worked in a warehouse, and I walked through the door yelling, Maria. I yelled, Maria, Maria, and then I saw her boss and said, Have you seen—but then I saw Maria by her side. Maria, I said, Thank—but she told me to shut up. She was frowning and pointing at the door and telling me to go outside. I'm sorry, she said, talking to her boss. This won't take long. I remember the sunlight, the way it danced, hovering, kissing, between her eyes, her cheek. I remember her teeth, the way she smiled. You left me, she said. Now, fuck off and die.

Horror is a door slamming. Horror is confusion and bewilderment and the message bank of a phone. Horror is waking in the middle of the night going over all that happened and wondering if it all *really* happened how you remember, and then asking why. Horror is lying awake and staring at the ceiling trying to place yourself in another's shoes, but being unable to, always walking to a point between understanding and despair. Horror is attempting to piece together the tiny fragments of your own life knowing you've lost too many pieces, but trying anyway, examining each one, turning them over and over, changing the angles, the titles, the tones, the locations, the characters, the fonts and moods as if, through inference, you might still be able to legitimize all that happened, as if it were possible to kid yourself that one day you might take all this pain and turn it into something meaningful between the covers of a book.

At some point, Microwave looked up and slapped the story against his palm. I don't know if it's horror, or what you call that, he said. But I call that a motherfucking story, bitch. It's not your classic horror, but that part about Thor damn nearly broke my heart. And when they caught you with drugs – very relatable. I smiled, briefly, told him thank you, and then listened while he told me about some of the stupid shit he had done when he was young, about the bongs he used to make using his parents' hose when he still lived at home, and about his dad who set up a homemade alarm around the garage because he was convinced those fucking dickhead young blokes next door were fucking with him, and about Slick Rick, this kid he used to know from school, who one day bet him that he couldn't drink five milks. Course this was back in the 60s, he said, when we had those clear glass milk half-pint bottles with the shiny aluminium lids. So you know what I said? I said, Fuck you, Slick Rick, and drank the milk in front of everyone. But then, ten minutes later, I vomited and shat all over the classroom floor. They called me Milky for a while, but one afternoon I punched Slick Rick in the face. Anyway, he said, getting up to leave. Not horror, but not bad. Let me know when you write the next one – and then he was gone.

At some point, I walked to the toilet and sat in the cubicle. I did my neck rotations; pushed my thumbs into the muscles behind my neck, and bit into my shirt. Then

I sat at my desk. I thought about that afternoon, the park I lay in afterwards and the planes I stared at while trying to breathe, and I thought if I could just write something about that breathing, about the way it felt, about my lungs that couldn't fill and how I just wanted them to fill, if I could just say one true sentence about the sky, the weight of it, how it almost felt like it was pushing down, if I could just get to the heart of it, could communicate something about the unknowing, how I didn't know where the pain came from, and I didn't know why Maria sent that text, because I just wanted to know, because if I knew then maybe I could understand what I'd done wrong and stop the pain from happening again, or maybe if I could just admit that I wasn't abandoning Maria but *everyone,* then a sentence might become a para-graph and I would be able to express myself over the course of a long story too, but I couldn't – each time I tried I scratched the words out immediately because the sentences seemed repulsive, dramatic, sentimental, and who even gives a fuck, I thought, finally, about your memories and your pain and your stupid fucking life.

Horror is self-harm and suicide and depression and falsehood and entrapment and fear and abandonment, but horror is also criticality, those stories we tell our-selves that eventually come true. For years, I put myself down, telling myself that this story did not matter, that I did not matter, that I was a terrible writer, that the world did not need more sadness, that beyond the sadness it was simply embarrassing, that even if I could write I would never be able to explain it properly, exactly how it happened, and then I would give up all over again, swearing, as if it were possible, that I would never write again.

But perhaps I was not ready to tell that story, the whole story, the real one; perhaps I was not ready to admit that horror had saved my life too.

This one hurts. That afternoon, when I received Maria's text message, I was not at home but at Central station, ready to take my own life – Platform 16, a day like any other: sunny, blue skies, thirty degrees, one of those faded days from Sydney postcards long ago. I stood at the edge of the platform, tears welling, hat down, shaking. I did not want to die, but I wanted, *needed* the pain to end, and the idea that I might regain control over myself or a part of myself or anything made me feel powerful, but standing before each oncoming train I froze because the practicality of it terrified me, and I wept because I had never felt more powerless or scared or pathetic or alone. I wept and I prayed with every fibre in my body that it still might be possible to change, but when I opened my eyes nothing was different and nothing would ever be different and I wept, then, out of cowardice and shame. I remember the yellow line blurring, children laughing, sunlight glinting against buildings above trees. I remember station staff blowing whistles, ordering me, once more, behind the line. It was just a step, I thought. Just one. In those final moments that stretched, seemingly, to eternity, I thought, suddenly, of myself as a little boy – seven years old, fancy dress day at school; my father had taken the sheepskin rug from home and tied it to my back and for an entire day I crawled around on my hands and knees – and, finally, I wept, then, for that tiny Oliver who had believed in transformation and magic, unable to understand how that boy had become me.

***

Perhaps you can understand why I've never told this story: not to friends, nor family, nor partners – the outline of it, maybe, but never the specifics, not the full story, the real one – beyond its unbelievability, its almost Hollywood-like plot, I kept it a secret out of shame, then soul-crushing fear. In the past, very occasionally, when I absolutely had to, I would tell the version of the story where I stood on the edge of the platform and saw sunlight and heard laughter; I would make it absolutely apparent that I did not want to die, but that I had run out of options; I would talk about walking forward, hearing the blow of the whistle, and then remembering myself as a little boy. Then I would look up with tears in my eyes, and they would say, But Oliver, you *didn't* jump. And then, with an arm around me, You *didn't*. And I would nod, repeating, I *didn't* jump, agreeing with the truth of it, while also knowing, deep down, that the truth was a total lie.

Because here's the part that buries me – I *would* have jumped; in another universe – I *did*. In that final moment, I was not saved by a sense of obligation to my family or friends. I was not thinking about rail workers or commuters looking on. I did not, suddenly, make peace with myself. The pain did not dissolve and the little boy inside me did not rearrange the world so I saw it anew. I had made my choice; I was ready, lost. I had broken. But in that final moment, I received a text message from a girl I loved that told me she was going to die, and I ran. No courage, nothing heroic – it was luck, timing; it was maths, pure and simple: I valued her life more than my own.

Five years wrestling with this story, and I still can't tell it chronologically because I don't understand it – because no matter how many ways I arrange the pieces it doesn't make sense. Because this is not a fiction – there are effects I cannot explain, and their causes haunt me. What happened? Why did you want to hurt me? Why? But then there are other nights where I wake at three in the morning and find myself deleting paragraphs, whole narratives, rearranging large blocks of text. Because all I want to do is say thank you. All I want to do is enclose the letter I wanted to write but could not write all those years ago –

Here's the truth: Horror can be beauty; horror can take the form of a joke, and jokes, even those malicious ones, can offer brief windows where mothers call their sons and pull them back from the dead.

Portals

At some point I just thought: fuck it. I was sick of being sad and I was sick of the pain and I was sick of being, or trying to be, a writer. I wanted to forget everything, or I wanted my old life, or a new one, or I wanted to forget.

Around that time I had been doing those boring announcements that told everyone where they were and where they were going but everyone always looked so shitty and sad. Everyone always looked so broken and lost whenever I announced the places they had to go – I wondered if I could do anything to help.

So one morning I said, Attention, customers, next stop is Normanhurst – named after . . . Harvey Normanhurst. Then, a short while later I said, Next stop is Eastwood – named after . . . Clint Eastwood. I told people that Homebush was named after war criminal turned painter George W. Bush and that the City of Sydney loved him so much they decided to name a station after him. Then I laughed and told people that's how easy it was. All you had to do was disappear for a while and turn to art and everyone would forget who you were.

But it wasn't until we pulled out of Central on the way to Revesby via the airport that I really knew what to do. It wasn't until the rain poured and the skyline began to fade and the rails reflected like quartz in the storm that I felt the words rise within me, and it wasn't until we entered a tunnel and Sydney turned black that I felt those words form sentences – and if you could have only been there when I started calling the office workers NAUGHTY, if you could have only heard my laugh then heard everyone laugh when I began addressing the naughty office workers who had left work early by haircut instead of name. Hey Short Back and Sides, I said. And then I told them I knew their game. It was 4.30 p.m. and we were approaching the airport and I told them they could pull fast ones on their bosses but they couldn't pull fast ones on me. All you loose units looking to party at the Gold Coast this weekend – next stop . . . domestic airport! Then I started giggling manically, quietly. I opened the doors and closed them. I gave the bell. I felt drunk, not on alcohol but power, ideas, promise. The train began to move and I picked up the intercom and said, Attention, party people, and all the CB Divas looking to escape to Bali for the long weekend – next stop . . . international airport!

And as we emerged from the tunnel I swear to God lightning cracked in the shape of a crucifix, and, for a second, I was just a child remembering how fun it was to make shit up.

Course, as a child, I'd been known to do dumb things before. When I was seven I stole a Crunchie Bar from the bottom of a filing cabinet. I was studying at Kumon – this Maths tutoring centre somewhere in Canberra – and that's where they kept their Crunchies and Snickers and Kit Kats – all the rewards for doing heaps well: in the bottom of a filing cabinet. I wasn't allowed chocolate at home. And I wanted a Crunchie real bad. So I got one. It was easy. I just put my hand in there and I got it.

On the way home Mum was like, How was your day? and I was like, Mmhmm. Then Mum said, What's in your mouth? and I was like, Mmhmm. Then Mum slammed on the brakes because I had chocolate all over my face. We went back to Kumon. Mum made me apologize to the smart students for eating their chocolate and to the teachers for losing their trust, and I cried and cried.

Later, after we got home, Dad lectured me about the importance of resolve and being honest. But he also paused and told me how life was about even more than that. How life was about detail, about paying attention to the details. He said, If you'd just remembered to wipe the chocolate off your face . . . you probably would have got away with it – almost smiling, the beginnings of a smile. So I swore then that I'd pay attention. I swore then that I'd try, because what else can we do other than try?

Except when it happened, when I purchased two packets of cigarettes from the kiosk at Vientiane's international airport in Laos, I wasn't thinking about any of that. It was only after, after I'd boarded the plane, that I had a chance to think about Thor.

Let me tell you about Thor:

When I was in year three I knew a kid named Thor. Thor was cool because he had a Nike swoosh earring and a rat-tail and said phrases like, Heaps feral, and Feral dick. Pretty much didn't matter what someone asked him, he'd just answer with, Heaps feral, or Feral dick.

About the same time Mum had given me the book *Where Do Babies Come From.* I was pretty curious about where babies came from and I read that book a lot. I learned about puberty. I learned about sex. I learned about things changing and growing and that babies come from vaginas, not bottoms.

One day Thor and I were on the playground, playing soccer and trying to score goals when the girls were watching. Thor started telling me how nothing could hurt him. He said, Don't have any pain receptors in me body. I squinted. He said, Go on, punch me, I dare ya. Then I didn't punch him, and he punched himself, and said, Told ya.

I was too busy trying to make eyes at this one girl I thought was cute. Her name was Rachel. I told Thor

I thought Rachel was cute and he said, Yeah, she's heaps feral, aye, while smiling. I could tell he agreed with me 'cause of how he never spoke to her and got real shy when she was around. I said, I think I'm gonna go talk to her, and then I went over to her.

But then I got nervous. My mouth went dry, and I didn't know what to say. I remembered my dad had said that girls liked intelligent guys who paid attention to the details, and that people get intelligent from reading books. So I decided I was going to tell her about the book I'd been reading. I decided I was going to tell her some details about the world.

So I tapped Rachel on the shoulder. I said, Wanna know something I learned about Ms Callaghan? She said, What? and I said, Ms Callaghan has a big vagina.

Then it was silent. Then Rachel screamed. She screamed like this: AHHHHHH.

And then she started running. She started running to the top of the playground and I started running and she began screaming, I'm telling! and I began screaming, Don't tell! and then I started saying then yelling, That's what happens to people when they grow up! and that I could explain, and that a book had told me.

But then I lost her. She was gone. I knew it was all over, that somehow everything was fucked and that I'd lost. That in year two I'd already lost.

Thor came up to me and asked what happened and I told him. I told him about puberty and people's bits growing and how Ms Callaghan was an adult with a big vagina, and he laughed, then punched me in the dick. He said, Feral dick.

I lay down on my back staring at the clouds, watching them move over each other, watching things change while also staying the same.

Twenty minutes later Ms Callaghan called me to her office. Thirty minutes later my parents were called. An hour later my parents were sitting next to me in the principal's office. The principal kept asking if Thor had put me up to it. Kept using the phrase, bad egg. I kept saying, Naa, and, No way. The principal asked why I'd said Ms Callaghan had a big vagina and I said, Because I learned it in a book! Because I learned it was true. The principal said nothing and I looked at my mum and she said, Well . . . it is, sort of, true.

The principal told me I had to apologize to Ms Callaghan so I went to the teachers' lounge. Ms Callaghan was crying. She asked me if I had anything to say and I said, I'm sorry I said you had a big vagina.

Then I left. School was finished. I saw Thor down by the road. A car pulled over and a man got out. Thor said, Hey, and the man said something, and Thor said something, and then the man slapped Thor upside the head. Hard. Thor covered his face with his hands, then wiped his eyes. Then I heard the man say, Get in the car ya fucking feral, and then Thor was in the car, and then they were gone.

And so now believe me when I tell you I wasn't thinking about my life and the dumb things I'd done when I emptied my pockets at the X-ray machine in Vientiane, Laos and saw a stick of weed on the blue examining tray next to my keys, and iPhone, and wallet. Believe me that when the baggage screening official looked at the stick of weed and back at me I wasn't thinking about the time I'd torn all the tendons in my ankle while working in a warehouse on the outskirts of Calgary because of lying about being able to drive a forklift, and not wearing steel-capped boots but skate shoes instead. That I wasn't thinking about the frostbite I got on seven toes while snowboarding in Argentina because I thought, maybe, I'd look tough wearing Converse shoes while partying at night in the snow. That I wasn't thinking about the lessons we learn and the choices we make and the way our choices can affect other people. This voice in my head and the voice saying: God damn it, Oliver. You fucking idiot. Believe me – I wasn't thinking. I wasn't thinking.

I wasn't thinking because when the baggage-screening official made eyes at me and at the bin behind her I was already having trouble breathing. A small amount of urine in my pants and my breath not breathing then going:

Breaaatheeeeee. Breaaatheeeeee. Breaaatheeeeee.

I wasn't thinking about Thor's car roaring down the road, and how I'd looked at my parents, and how I'd felt lucky. I wasn't thinking about Thor's dad and how it had seemed unfair, then, that we would grow into larger versions of ourselves. I wasn't thinking about any of that because all I could think about were the thousands of cameras in the airport and however many cameras were above me. My hand, now viewed from above, moving in slow motion as I picked up the weed and dropped it in the bin.

And sitting in the smoking room inhaling cigarette after cigarette I waited for them to come. And I imagined them moving up the stairs. Mobilizing. The smoking room: fluorescent lights and nothing and my dumb body existing within it. And so then I closed my eyes. And inside my head I saw them coming. And I imagined how I wouldn't fight them. Because you do things you don't mean to and things happen. I imagined how they'd gather in the terminal beyond the windowpane and how I'd drop my cigarette into the ashtray and how they'd stare at me and how I'd stare back. Staring – that moment I'd look back on in the future to realize how *truly* nothing matters except when you're letting other people down, how you didn't pay attention.

For some reason they didn't come. My plane was called and I got on the plane and the plane took off and we left into the sky and I did too. And I thought about Thor and his dad and his mum and his dad's dad and his dad's mum and his mum's mum and his mum's dad. And I thought about my mum and my dad and my mum's mum and my mum's dad and my dad's dad and my dad's mum: larger versions of ourselves already existing and telling us to follow – everyone fucking up and meaning to or not. And I prayed a little prayer not to God but to myself. I prayed: let me pay attention to the details, for life truly hurts when we hurt those closest to us without ever meaning to. And I hoped that I would. That I'd pay attention. But I also knew that people were people and that I was one of them. And that there are some things you can't change. I knew that. I did.

But I also knew something else: that in the future I'd hear the soldiers coming – quietly at first, but then not: all metal and guns and smiling and knives, marching, louder, louder.

And so now I ask you to close your eyes.

Can you hear them?

They're coming for you too.

Not horror, I hear Microwave saying, grinning, but not bad. But perhaps, now, I think, it was horror – because I wrote a story where I prophesied my own pain and that story came true.

Notebook

I have bought a new notebook to try and tell this story, this last story, once and for all. Normally, I despise those fancy, leather-bound notebooks that first-year writing students clutch to their chests or use to jot down the notes or fragments of conversations from the lives of others, but this notebook, while appearing to be leather, is not leather, is a shitty plastic, and across the front is the word NOTEBOOK in a gold trim that has already, at least partially, begun to disappear, which is to say that this shitty notebook is the perfect container for the story I have written then rewritten then abandoned many times before, but that I will now, hopefully, finally, try to salvage or rearrange so that I can put this story behind me and never look at it again.

But it doesn't help, nothing does. I've spent weeks, now months, writing this story from different angles, trying to return to the heart of it, to those final months on the railway where I barely spoke to anyone, preferring, instead, to keep to myself, to perform the job exactly as had been drilled into us, to make announcements, which I performed mechanically, listlessly, and to ensure the safe running of the train. But what I keep ruining is the tone: I can't get across the self-resentment I felt. I hurt people close to me, then my body broke down, again, and I blamed myself for it. I begged for the pain to stop, but I also told myself I deserved it, and it scared me. I can't get across *that* fear.

In the afternoons on my days off, or in the late morning after night shift, I would run from my house down Abercrombie Street, past Café Ella, Shortlist, the Glengarry, glancing briefly at my phone, knowing it would hurt, but doing it anyway, pressing play to David August's essential mix, not because I particularly liked David August or the essential mix, but because my brother had recommended it, loved it, and because sometimes when I ran and listened to his music I felt we were running together, that he in Hobart and I in Sydney were, in fact, running in some fictitious, alternative place where pain didn't exist and teleportation was possible.

But I also ran because, for a long time, running was the only thing that took the pain away. In those early days I ran for fifteen, then twenty minutes at a time, and afterwards I would stumble home, pale, coughing up phlegm, but happy, briefly, to be out of my head, knowing that the pain would return, but celebrating, privately, those small wins, as if some alchemic process were occurring, which, in fact, on a cellular level, it was.

However, what I remember most, now, about those early runs were the conversations I had with my sister afterwards, where I would call and she would tell me about the pain clinics she had begun contacting, and the pain-specific psychologists she had begun researching, and sometimes when she asked how I was I would tell her I was okay and I would not even have to lie.

One afternoon, three quarters of the way along the coastal track from Bondi to Coogee, the running became too much; my normal breathing turned rapid, uncontrollable and, suddenly, I found myself unable to breathe. The horror, at least immediately, was not that I was having a panic attack, but rather that somebody, or worse somebody I knew, would see, and so I stumbled down to Gordon's Bay and hid behind a rock where I hyperventilated aggressively into my shirt. When I returned to the path, the sun had gone down and I walked through the streets of Clovelly until I found a bus stop. I sat, then, and began to pray.

Know this: pain, although especially chronic pain, has a way of unhinging you – life as you know it evaporates, and what remains resembles a joke or cruel magician's trick where you try to heal yourself or pretend you have already healed, but instead you continually saw yourself in half, the only difference being that the screams, or internal screams, are real, and that there is no audience and no applause, and you have no control over when the next act might be or how long it will last.

All these years, and still I can't find the words to tell you what happened next – that when I opened my eyes I saw a sign, a literal sign across the road. Because how do you do that? How do you write about the profound? The miraculous? How do you tell people the truth without sounding like a total fraud? Even now, even though it *happened*, even though it *saved* me, the writer in me hates it – this cliché narrative where prayers are unexpectedly answered, where boys in pain open their eyes and see this across the road:

ARE YOU IN PAIN?
ROLFING CAN HELP!

BACK PAIN
NECK PAIN
SHOULDER PAIN
HEADACHES
MIGRAINES
BAD POSTURE

But now, I wonder whether the writer in me hates it for another reason: because, even though the pain was horrific, the writer in me is terrified that without that narrative we will struggle, again, to write, to stay alive.

The fuck is a ROLFER? my brother asked. Like a ROFLCOPTA? I'd called him and told him about the run and the prayer and the sign, and then I told him I didn't know. All I knew was that I'd prayed and received a sign. Well, Bear said. If you're not listening to the signs, you're stepping on the mines. It's probably a scam, I said, laughing, but—Listen to the signs! Bear said. So then I asked if he could help me look it up. I told him I'd look it up but—Bear just told me he knew. Don't worry, he said. I got you! And then, after a moment, he announced that he'd found the ROLF DADDY. ROLFING, he said, is a form of alternative medicine originally developed by Ida Rolf as Structural Integration. It is typically delivered as a series of ten hands-on physical manipulation sessions sometimes called *The Recipe*. Typically, the recipe involves the manipulation of the fascia and soft tissue to create better alignment and balance in the body—Well, I don't know what the hell that means, Bear said, but I reckon if someone's giving you the recipe . . . you cook it. I'm going to cook it, I told Bear. That's my guy, Bear said. Put PAPA ROLF in the deep fryer.

That night, squinting, and then with my eyes closed, I made an appointment and the following morning I performed my mostly useless neck rotations in the shower. I kept telling myself that everything would be okay. I kept telling myself it was probably a scam but maybe it wasn't and then I told myself I was tough. I told myself so many people would have given up by now, but not you. I told myself that the pain had gone once and the pain could go again and then I looked at myself in the mirror and told myself I was brave. I closed my eyes and told the voices in my head to go away and then I opened my eyes and made a promise to believe. I saw my reflection in the mirror and my reflection saw me back and we made a promise to try just one more time – we knew it was stupid and we knew it was dumb but if we could just try one more time, if we could just hold on, if we could just shut up and pretend to love one another then maybe everything would go away and one day we would even learn to like each other too.

But how do we talk about narrative and abandonment? How do we talk about those promises we made to keep our story alive? One night Maria turned to me and said, Promise me you'll never leave. I promise, I said, laughing. No, she said. Like you mean it – everyone always leaves and if we're going to do this I need you to mean it. I promise, I said again. I do. But those were early days – I had never considered, even for a moment, that I would abandon myself too.

For many years that paragraph or the idea of that paragraph haunted me, and over the course of six years I abandoned this project more times than I know. The pain seemed too large, too unknowable, and beyond that

I did not know how to record or attempt to record all that happened. I did not know how to handle the trauma or the relived trauma, and I did not know how to cope with the knowledge that through the process of writing so much would be lost. No one's expecting you to reproduce reality exactly as it happened, my father said, one afternoon. That would be impossible, and besides, writers write because they want to tell a story, to take people on a journey, because they want to entertain. But what if I don't want to entertain? I replied, nervously. What if I simply want to understand? And then, silently, What if I simply want to be understood?

The man was handsome and lived in a mansion and my first thought was to run. The whole picture, everything, was too obvious. I didn't trust his beard and I didn't trust his feet and I didn't trust his voice – it was too calm, soothing, or perhaps I was so terrified of what I would do if this didn't work out that it was all I could do not to run. But instead we shook hands and I followed him to his studio that overlooked the ocean at the back of the house.

Then we sat and I said something stupid like, Business must be good! and he smiled and handed me a piece of paper and told me to fill it out, but I told him I couldn't. I wanted to fill it out, but I couldn't, or I could but it would hurt. Then I told him I didn't want to hurt. I scrunched up my face and looked at the ground and told him my head hurt and my neck hurt and my back hurt and my face had even started hurting too. Like little electrocutions, I said, but slower – and my jaw, I can barely chew. He shifted in his chair and asked how long this had all been going on for and I told him, Years . . . on and off for years, and I tried to smile. I told him about the ten-month-migraine and the Healer and how the migraine had gone, but how it had come back. I told him how I couldn't read or write or look at screens and how for a long time I couldn't sit. I had to relearn how to sit, I said, but even now, if I sit for too long—I told him how mostly I kept it a secret or tried to keep it a secret, that before I worked for the trains I did drugs because they were fun and because everyone did drugs and because, at least for a while, they took take the pain away. But now they drug-test, I said, so I can't really self-medicate – all I can do is run. I told him my friend Sam thought the trains were the best thing to ever happen to me. I love it, he'd say. It's like you're in state-sponsored rehab! But he doesn't know how bad it is; no one does, and now I can't do anything, and no one knows why. No one can help. I can't—and then I asked if he understood or if any of this made sense. I knew it didn't make sense and I just wanted it to make sense and I stared at the floor and told myself I wouldn't cry. I'd been doing better, I said, trembling; I thought it was over. At some point I forced a smile and pointed at the massage table and said, Well—but he just put a hand on my shoulder and told me it was okay, to slow down. There's no rush, he said. Just be yourself. For a while, I sat, unable to talk.

I remember a murky, heavy roaring in my stomach, then chest. I know you're hurting, he said. I can see you're scared, but you're okay. You're okay, he said, again, his hand still on my shoulder, tears welling in the corner of my eyes. You're okay. I know you don't want to cry, but you can. It's okay.

I don't remember how long I sat there, but eventually I composed myself and we moved to the massage table where he began working on my neck and back and head. You're in pain, he said. I know that – and then he spoke about posture, fascia and alignment, about the ways our bodies change and grow, and how he had been in pain once and all the absurd treatments he had gone through to find relief. Then he asked if I was a perfectionist. I told him I didn't know, probably not, that when I was younger my dad was always telling me how to pack the dishwasher correctly, that even now my room was a disaster, that I always had food stains on my clothes. But then I said, I guess with writing, you know, before, when I could do it – I was obsessive. I told him my sentences had to sound a certain way, that I did not have synaesthesia, but that I could imagine seeing them like colours, that paragraphs were music, that when I read sentences, or my sentences, I saw, in my mind, the image of horses galloping, or jumping, or cantering, but one wrong word, one wrong note, I knew, could create in the ground a depression so severe that those horses might stumble, and if one horse stumbled there was a chance they all might stumble, and fall, and then, in the crowds, there would be riots. Okay, he said. And do you consider yourself a people pleaser? Do you care if people like you? I don't know, I said, but then, after a while, I guess I care tremendously about what people think.

For the rest of the session we continued in silence, and towards the end I even felt a little better, but when we returned to his desk he said, Oliver – I want to thank you for coming in. I know this is expensive, and you can continue seeing me if you found this useful, but I don't think I can help. I remember a sinking feeling, then hearing him say, But I might know someone who can, and forcing, hard, a smile. I felt embarrassed, defeated. I had cried, again, and I suppose, for a moment, I had believed or almost believed in that dirty word called hope – I had believed in signs and strangers and prayers being answered; I had believed, foolishly, that I had been heard.

I know you can't read, he said, but I want you to read a book. A book, I said, and then, regrettably, I asked if he wrote it. But he just smiled and said No, that it had been written by a doctor in the early 90s, that the book had cured thousands of people with chronic pain and that based on our conversation he thought the book might help me too, and then he paused and said that it was almost funny, the way I was looking – it was the same look he'd had when he'd been suffering and the book had been given to him.

Listen: this part, even though it shouldn't, embarrasses me. I never knew how I would write it. The idea, I suppose, that all my pain, or at least all my chronic migraines and headaches, jaw pain and back pain, might be solved by a book always seemed too neat or unbelievable or hokey or convenient, and on a narrative level it seemed, at least to me, unacceptable to express that even though writing a book had triggered my chronic pain, it would, in the end, be a book that solved it. Likewise, on a personal level, the idea seemed abhorrent, and for many weeks after leaving the ROLFER I rejected it, preferring, instead, to continue running, to continue doing neck rotations in the shower, to continue lying on my thumbs which I pushed, painfully, deeply, into my neck and when that stopped working to purchase massage sticks, to spend exorbitant amounts of money on masseuses, chiropractors, foam rollers, to purchase, eventually, absurdly, something called a Neck Hammock, which I set up in my bedroom and suspended my neck and head – it seemed, for no discernible reason – in a plastic sheath several centimetres above the ground, to continue being in pain, to continue treating my pain as a structural issue, as something that could be manipulated and repaired.

One evening, two weeks later, waiting for the driver to arrive so we could prepare a train at Auburn Maintenance Centre, I sat, shifting in my chair, staring at the ceiling then staring at the floor – I couldn't look at the TV and I couldn't look at the lights and I couldn't read books and I held my breath because I couldn't do it any more. I couldn't live with the hurt and the fear and I couldn't look at my phone, and I just wanted to look at my stupid phone. I just wanted to text someone or read something and to not be in pain. I was so sick of being in pain. I was so sick of no one being able to help and no one understanding, and I just wanted answers, something to happen – I *needed* something to change.

So I removed my wallet and glanced at the paper with the doctor's name and the doctor's book and my head began to throb, and I imagined reading the book or *any* book and then I imagined staring at my iPad and downloading the book and my head throbbed even harder. It throbbed so hard that I can still feel it *now*. Then I closed my eyes and my breath drew short because I knew I would do it and I knew it would hurt and I knew this meant something or everything because I no longer cared or I cared so deeply that I was willing – and how do I tell you that I prayed, then, with every fibre in my being, that this wasn't just hippy, pseudo-science bullshit, that the ROLFER might be right and that this wouldn't be like last time, that this book might allow me to heal.

Picture this: a grown man trembling under fluorescent lights looking at his iPad then looking away, squinting, holding his own hands beneath the table, trying to breathe. Even now, I cannot tell you how I stared at the screen long enough to download the book and glance at its first few pages, but I suppose I was so desperate for help that I willed, at least for those first minutes, the pain to remain level, manageable – I kept telling myself that everything would be okay. Besides, I thought, it was just reading, and then I even tried to smile because it was almost funny when you thought about it: needing to read a book to alleviate pain when reading was the activity that caused it.

And it was almost funny, too, when the driver arrived and said, Jesus, mate. You're a sight for sore eyes! Hey! How much overtime have you done? Chuck a sickie tomorrow, you poor cunt, and get some fucking sleep! It was almost funny when the book said to resume physical activity and that even though the pain would hurt and for a while might even get worse, the pain would not harm and I almost started laughing when after we prepared the train I sat in my guard compartment and the book told me to start talking to my pain too. The book told me to tell my brain that I wouldn't take it any more so I said, I won't take it any more, and then I really did laugh because it seemed so pathetic and tragic and fucked up: the ideas people put into books to make money and the hopeless people who bought them. I won't take it, I said again, feeling stupid, but saying it louder, my head cracking, splitting, but smiling, or trying to smile – if Maria were here, I thought, she'd find it funny: the way we keep our pain a secret; the way we let it out – I won't take it. At some point my breathing turned rapid and the head veins began to pop, but I choked out another laugh and shook my head and massaged my temples and cleared my throat and rubbed the sweat from my eyes and kept telling myself I was okay. I kept reading that the pain wasn't pain but the pain was a symptom or oxygen deprivation, but then I couldn't see because there were tears in my eyes. I couldn't see because my hands kept shaking and my head kept throbbing and my skull kept breaking and then the whole world was breaking and nothing helped and nothing ever helped and I dropped the iPad on to the seat beside me and sat on my hands and wept.

At some point the driver gave the bell, and I returned it, and we pulled out of the maintenance centre on the way to the city. Empty train, no stops, twenty minutes to Central – I remember breathing, deliberately, slowly, passing Strathfield, Burwood, then yelling ridiculously, wholeheartedly, for help. It may seem comical now, but at the time it felt deadly serious, and I held my head while looking up then down then right then left as I completed those hopeless eye exercises that an optometrist had taught me long ago. And then I remember looking at myself in the reflection of the window and knowing with absolute certainty that if I did not try again or try harder or try differently I would die. It was a feeling, nothing more, but the weight of it shook me, and as I stared at the red and green and yellow lights of the signals and the light rain that began to fall and the passing trains and all those people seated and pushed up against one another staring at the books and phones in their laps, I began repeating in my head, and then faintly, as a whisper, Please.

What happened next, like most of this story, defies logic, but in the minutes that followed I read, in disbelief, as Dr Sarno described the moment my pain began. He wrote:

> People often report that at the moment of onset they hear some kind of noise, a crack, a snap, a pop. Patients often use the phrase 'my back went out'. They are sure that something has broken. In fact, nothing breaks, but the patient will swear that there has been some kind of structural damage. The noise is a mystery. It may be that it is similar to the noise elicited by the manipulation of the spine, which is a kind of 'cracking the knuckles' of the joints of spinal bones. One thing is clear – the noise indicates nothing harmful. Though the low back is the most common location for an acute attack, it can occur anywhere in the neck, shoulders, or upper and lower back. Wherever it occurs, it is the most painful thing I know of in clinical medicine, which is ironic because it is completely harmless.

And how do I tell you, now, what it meant to read that paragraph then? How do I tell you that after countless doctors, healers or people who claimed they could heal, *no one* had *ever* explained that initial breaking, that snapping, that *pop*?

In April 2016, shortly after my first recovery or partial recovery with the Healer, I wrote about the onset of my pain for *Rolling Stone Australia,* and in the piece I used the words:

> . . . but then I couldn't focus on the screen any more because the pain had grown into PAIN and oh fuck it felt like something inside my head was stretching and breaking and stretching and breaking and stretching and breaking and stretching and stretching and then: something broke. Or it felt like it did. I don't know. I walked to the park and vomited. Next to me there was a car with the bumper sticker that said: WINE ME/DINE ME/69 ME. I lay on my back and cried.

In that *Rolling Stone Australia* piece, a character much like myself was attempting to write a story he had titled *The Most Beautiful Story In The World* about a couple who had been trying, without much luck, to fall pregnant, but then the author mysteriously suffered a migraine that rendered him incapable, physically, of finishing the story. In reality, at the onset of my migraine, I had been sitting for several weeks attempting a grant application that I would never complete to produce my second book, raising and lowering my laptop to different heights, convinced the machine's angle, the screen's glare was responsible for the growing, then deafening pain in my head, until, one glorious afternoon, something in my head, or neck, snapped or popped – it was audible, and I stumbled outside to the park next door and vomited on the grass.

That evening, passing Newtown then Macdonaldtown, I read anxiously, feverishly, Dr Sarno's message: that repression of unconscious rage and guilt, usually through the desire to please others or be perfect, manifests in the body as pain, which is caused by mild oxygen deprivation via the autonomic nervous system, and that by acknowledging the psychosomatic origins of the pain, symptoms usually clear up because they no longer have reason to exist.

As we arrived at Central, the pain, unbelievably, however minutely, began to lift, and while I dared not celebrate I did smile, briefly, recognizing Microwave at the end of the platform waiting to relieve my train. Big night on the gear, mate? he said, winking, and then, Christ – looks like you've seen a ghost. I can't imagine how I must have looked – those bloodshot eyes, that smile, or almost smile, although I recognize now that I was probably in a state of shock – it seemed shocking, suddenly, after so many years, to see myself as a character in the story of another, to realize that my pain story wasn't special, that there were others like me, that, perhaps, there might even be someone who could help, who could show me, from beyond the grave, a path through which I might heal.

***

The book was not a magic bullet. The following day the pain returned, as the book said it might, but I just read and reread Dr Sarno's *Healing Back Pain* as if it were a bible, and alone in my train carriage, I spent that day – and most days for the next three months – talking, then yelling at myself as if I were a madman. I would close my doors and make my announcements and yell at the pain to go away, and when that didn't work I would go online and tell myself the screen couldn't hurt me and read other people's pain stories too. I would read about Ted who had severe pain in both legs for eight years and who had been diagnosed with, as he wrote, everything under the sun: chondromalacia, adolescent patellofemoral syndrome, severely pronated feet, childhood arthritis and, eventually, fibromyalgia, until, one day, a family member heard Howard Stern talking about Dr Sarno on the radio, and a year later, after meeting with Dr Sarno and reading his books the pain was gone. I would read about Sherri who had back pain for twenty years, and all the various doctors she would see that were able to offer temporary relief, but never a cure, that would hold her until the next devastating episode where she would repeat the process all over again, until one day she heard Dr Sarno on the radio and, after reading his books, the pain, within a month, had vanished. I would read about Jim the magician who couldn't perform magic because his back stopped working and about Drew who couldn't run because his knees started buckling and about Mia who couldn't sleep or leave her bed because her head hurt so badly that she wanted to die – there were thousands of people with back pain and neck pain and hip pain and knee pain and sciatica pain and migraines and headaches and chronic fatigue syndrome and irritable bowel syndrome and repetitive strain injuries and eczema and even other gastrointestinal and chronic pain symptoms too, and no one could help them but now they had healed, and when my head hurt so much I couldn't stare at the screen I would type: DR SARNO PAIN STORIES into YouTube and close my eyes and force a smile and tell myself to *believe*.

Other times, though, I would do nothing more than sit quietly and think about the psychological reasons the pain had existed in the first place, about that absurd desire to please others or be perfect, and while I could not forgive myself, then, for betraying myself and certain people I had loved, I tried to stare into that guilt to understand myself and those reasons for the terrible things I had done.

But here's the thing about pain: it does not simply vanish; we do not simply read a book and make the bad things go away.

A month before I quit, I went to a psychother-apist. Beyond a tight neck, miraculously, Dr Sarno had sent the physical pain away, but in its place I felt a gaping anxiety or fear or anger that sometimes or a lot of the time made it hard to breathe and I wanted to know why people hurt one another and why people hurt them-selves. I wanted to know why my body had failed and why most of my relationships had failed and I wanted to know how not to fail again. I had given up on psycholo-gists, but the book said somatic psychotherapists might be of help, and since the book had proved miraculous, I took a bus out west.

In the living room of a single-storey terrace I sat and told a lady about my pain and she asked me to tell her the story of my life. I told her I'd had a good childhood. Lov-ing, supportive parents – no trauma, no abuse. There was that one time when I was eight and this fifteen-year-old invited me into his garage and rode around, I guess, mas-turbating on a bike, but nothing happened, not really, and besides, I said, compared to what other people go through I was almost lucky. Then I told her I was too busy hang-ing out with Dean and Melanie to worry about that anyway. We rode our bikes to the BMX track and skated in the street and Melanie and I even had our first kiss before she moved away, but then my family was moving away too. I told her I was nine and we moved to Texas and it was probably stupid but everyone went through puberty so young and I didn't understand why everyone looked older than I did. Everyone had hair under their arms and hair on their legs and was obsessed with religion and sex and Abercrombie & Fitch and I felt like a child. I was a child, but I wanted to be like them, and I remember doing push-ups and sit-ups and jumping exercises in the garage. I wanted to be stronger and taller and bigger and better—I don't know why I'm telling you any of this, I said. It's not like I got beat up or anything. I had a few friends; we played basketball and went to church, but mostly, I guess, I just felt ignored. Then I even laughed or tried to laugh and said, I actually wrote a book about it a few years ago, but the day it came out I—and then I stared at the floor. My stomach felt hot and I drank a glass of water and the lady told me that everything would be okay. It's okay, she said. This is a safe space. And then, after a while she said, Perhaps you could tell me a bit more about your parents? So then I nodded and told her my mum was one of the kindest, most generous people I had ever met. She was a psychologist and I probably told her too many problems but she always listened and was always there. And my dad, I said, was one of the most capable, practical men I had ever known, and I always wanted to be just like him. I told her he used to be an army man, and when I was younger I used to imagine I was Rambo. I didn't know what an army man did but I imagined it was like Rambo and I used to tie one of his ties around my head and feel powerful and strong—but during the migraine, I said, the first one, the ten-month one, they—they weren't there and I wanted to write but I couldn't write and I felt so useless and weak and I know I was twenty-five and you need to grow up and you can't rely on your parents but I just wished they were there and

I felt hurt and alone and it's not even rational because I couldn't use a phone and I couldn't tell them but I also didn't want to worry them because each day I knew it couldn't last much longer and I kept telling myself it would get better but each day it got worse and—and besides, I said, after a moment. I had Maria. Then the lady told me to take a breath and she refilled my glass and asked who Maria was and I told her that too. I told her she was my eyes. I told her maybe we were in love or maybe we weren't but maybe it didn't matter. I told her we slept and we cooked and we ate and we fucked, and that in the beginning, despite the pain, we had fun, that we played games, but after a while it felt like all we did was cry. I would hold her, taking more painkillers trying to keep my own pain together, but after months and months I just couldn't do it. I was so fried and weak and hollow and I wanted to be there but I couldn't be there I—no one else was there and I needed her because my eyes didn't work and my head didn't work and no one could help but a lot of the time I was the one that was helping her too. We helped each other but we needed each other but sometimes when I went to work there were sixty missed calls on my phone or messages and I couldn't read them and she knew I couldn't read them and I was trying to support us both on a casual job and when I got home she'd ask why I didn't answer and I'd tell her I couldn't answer because I was working and I was trying to help us both the best I could. Then my housemates said she had to move out and I lent her money and years later I found out she'd told her new housemates I was lying and stealing but I'd never done anything like that, not to her—I just wanted her to be okay. And then we broke up and she tried to have a threesome with my friends and she started sending me messages that Siri had to read about killing herself and I would meet her in the park and she would show me the knife and she would show me how she would do it and she would say that she loved me but if we didn't get back together she would do it and I didn't love her but I believed her and I knew if anything happened to her I would never forgive myself and she knew it too and I felt so fucked up and scared and confused and alone because I couldn't trust her and I couldn't trust myself and I didn't want anyone to die. The last time I spoke to her I didn't speak to her at all. At the airport, waiting for my plane back to Brisbane, I called her because she owed me money and I wanted to know when she would pay me, but I also hadn't heard from her for a while and I wanted to know if she was okay and to say goodbye. But when she answered it wasn't her, it was a boy. He asked who it was and I told him and he laughed and in the background I heard Maria laugh too. I said, Can you put Maria on? and he said, She isn't here, and I said, Just cut the bullshit, I can hear her laughing, and he said, Wait, are you the guy who lent her money? and I said, Just put her on the phone, and he said, Yeah, she tried to borrow money from me, but I guess I'm not a fucking idiot like you, and then I heard her laughing some more. Just put her on the phone, I said, again, but he just said, How about no, and hung up the phone—

I stared at the floor, breathing, or trying to breathe, trying not to cry, but then she said, What if Maria was simply doing the best she could? The question hung in the air as I turned it over and over in my head—but she didn't have to—what if she were simply doing the very best she could? She had a shitty childhood and people hurt her but that doesn't mean—what if she was simply doing the very, very best she could? I hung my head, then, and quietly began to sob. You always have a choice, I said, sobbing harder. For a long time I didn't understand how you could do that to someone – how you could hurt someone so deliberately, but then I lied and cheated on the last two people I dated, and I'd never done that before, ever; I'd prided myself on having a moral compass, on having integrity, but I'm just as fucked up as everybody else.

And what if you were simply doing the very best you could too? Then it wouldn't be good enough, I said, because I hurt other people and it sounds like an excuse. Oliver, she said. Look at me – you're not a bad person. How do you know? I said, meeting her eyes, tears streaming down my face. How do you know? Because I know. How? Because you're sitting in my office and you're burying your soul. Evil people bury souls all the time, I'm sure, I said, trying to smile, but sobbing harder, and for a while, we sat, her passing me tissues, until eventually I said, quietly, I just have so much hurt inside me, and I don't want to hurt any more. Have you forgiven her? She was there for me and she helped me—but you haven't forgiven her. No, I said, shaking my head, clutching my waist, my stomach, feeling a hot—could you forgive her? I don't know, I said, almost whispering, there were other things, worse—but if she were doing the best she could . . . could you forgive her? I suppose I would have to, I said, burying my face in my hands. I would—I would almost—and do you think you could forgive yourself too? But at this, I continued shaking my head. No, I said, because I wasn't—do you think you could forgive yourself for being in pain? For the ten-month migraine? For failing? Because your body was doing the best it could? And then I just started nodding, sobbing and nodding. I was just trying to do the best I could, I said, but—I know, she said. I was just trying to hold it together but my head kept—and then she told me the body was always talking to us. She told me my body was just trying to tell me something the only way it knew how, and I kept sobbing, saying, I know. And then she asked if my body was talking to me now. I told her my stomach. I pointed at my stomach and told her it felt hot, like a searing heat, and she asked if I could hold it. So I returned my hands to my stomach and the heat jumped and danced, and then she asked if I could speak my forgiveness aloud. So I closed my eyes and saw Maria and I saw myself and even now, all these years later, I hold my stomach and I still see us now. We're young, impossibly so, and we're sitting at Manly staring at the beach, smiling and eating fish and chips and laughing because the future hasn't happened and the past has been forgotten and there's a chance, even a slight one, that we might be falling in love. I forgive you, I said, softly, my hand shaking, pressing, remembering her face, her smile—I forgive you, I said, again, seeing my own eyes, downcast, my crumpled body in the corner of a shower, my body at platform 16, Central station, my hands pressing into my head, my neck, my temples, my voice, begging—I forgive you. And then she said, I know it's hard, but you must forgive yourself for the hurt you caused others too, and I saw their faces and the heat stabbed and rose and I whispered, I'm sorry, and then I saw the little boy inside me and I said sorry to him too. They may not forgive you, she said, but you must forgive you, and finally, between short, sharp breaths, I saw the wretched figure of a man I cut then and I forgave or tried to forgive myself too, and the heat rose and scalded through my stomach and ribcage and throat and finally, unable to do much else, I leant forward heaving and, uncontrollably, wept.

Listen: sometimes I want to erase them, these memories, these stories. Sometimes, in my notebook, they're almost illegible, like they're trying to disappear. But then I make out a sentence, a paragraph, and I'm a child once more. Grandmothers are angels and angels are real. Migraines don't exist and I am strong. And I realize these stories aren't stories but portals to the places that are no longer here, and we pass through them searching for people who were stronger than we were, searching for the glimpses of ourselves before everything went wrong.

Six years working on this book, and I still can't tell it right. Because I'm not telling you about the emergencies and those train passengers who became heroes, about the lady who collapsed in her seat and the people who gathered around her, the lady who said, Give her space, ordering strangers to call an ambulance while she put the lady in the recovery position and kept whispering, It's okay. Everything's going to be okay. I'm not telling you about the man who was so high he could not stand, could only smile while he slid down the wall on a platform at Central and the stranger who sat with him asking whether he'd had a good night while holding his hand so he did not fall on to the track. I'm not telling you about the lady who called me on the intercom and said, A BIRD JUST FLEW INTO THE TRAIN LIKE A SUPERMAN and the series of birdcalls she attempted to help the bird out, and I'm not telling you about the three teenagers on scooters who were listening to Kerser while accompanying an elderly woman to sit next to my crew compartment door because she was being abused by a man who was drunk.

But that doesn't even scratch the surface because I'm not telling you about the driver who used to change ends of the train using a cane and dark glasses and arriving at his door would ask a stranger, with a smile, what platform he was on and whether he could unlock the train door with his keys. I'm not telling you about the guard who loved the trains so much he citizen's-arrested any-one who infringed the rules and about the guard who was not fired but had a restraining order put on him because he punched our CEO in the face.

I'm not telling you about the beauty, what it felt like to be alone at 4 a.m. with my head not hurting listening to a mix by Thomas Gray and Liam Ebbs watching the world grow faint in orange and pink as we departed from Leppington or arrived at Richmond or made our way from the far reaches of the network back to the city.

I'm not telling you how gradually, regaining confi-dence, I made jokes over the intercom and wrote them down as if it might be possible to turn announcements into literature, as if it might be possible to say, then read: Mind the edge, ledge. And, If you're alighting . . . no fighting, in the pages of a book.

But most of all I'm not telling you how, sometimes, if you're paying attention, if you're really listening, the trains will tell their own stories. They'll tell you about a boy who had a migraine and how he nearly took his life once, but then they'll say: that's nothing special – look at us all together; there are millions of people, and they're all just like you.

***

After my last shift I went to see my boss and we sat in his office and I returned my shirts and pants and hats and whistle and belts and vests and flags and backpack and shoes and keys. My boss grinned. Can't believe you're quitting on me, mate! No one quits this job – but you want to be a writer . . . is that it? Yeah, I said. Do you think you'll write about the trains? I don't know, I said, smiling. Maybe. Well if you do, make sure you put me in it – make me tall and handsome and tell everyone I'm the best boss you ever had! I laughed, then, and told him I would. And when do you fly out to Spain? In a couple of days, I said. Well good luck, buddy, he said, shaking my hand. I hope you find what you're looking for.

And leaving that office I really hoped that I would, that one day I would make sense of all that happened or seemed to have happened, or if that were impossible that I would, at the very least, get out of my own way and take all these fragments and pick up a pencil and have the courage to try. More than anything, I suppose, I wanted for that: the courage, once more, to pick up a pencil and, wholeheartedly and hopelessly, try.